IMPERIAL WAR MUSEUM REVIEW

ARTICLES ON ASPECTS OF
TWENTIETH CENTURY HISTORY
LARGELY BY THE STAFF OF
THE IMPERIAL WAR MUSEUM

PUBLISHED BY
THE TRUSTEES OF
THE IMPERIAL WAR MUSEUM
GENERAL EDITOR:
JANET MIHELL
HISTORICAL EDITOR:
PETER SIMKINS
COVER DESIGN AND MAPS BY
JULIA MILLS
PRINTED BY
BLACK BEAR PRESS LIMITED

BRITISH LIBRARY CATALOGUING-IN-PUBLICATION DATA
A CATALOGUE RECORD FOR THIS BOOK IS AVAILABLE
FROM THE BRITISH LIBRARY
ISBN 1 870423 43 7

Cover illustration: Anthony Gross, *Troops moving through Maastricht, Holland, October 1944.* LD 4819

Contents

Lloyd George, the generals and the Palestine campaign, 1917–1918

Matthew Hughes

This article evaluates whether David Lloyd George's pursuit of a military campaign in Palestine from June 1917 to October 1918 was a sensible strategy for helping Britain defeat the Central Powers. It also examines the question of whether the 'generals'—notably William Robertson, the Chief of the Imperial General Staff (CIGS)—were disingenuous in the reports and evaluations they gave to the Prime Minister, with the purpose of destroying Lloyd George's plan to pursue campaigns in peripheral war zones away from the main fighting in France and Belgium.

The Palestine Campaign, June to December 1917

In his *War Memoirs* Lloyd George remarked how before General Edmund Allenby left for Egypt to assume command of the Egyptian Expeditionary Force (EEF) in June 1917 :

> I told him in the presence of Sir William Robertson that he was to ask us for such reinforcements and supplies as he found necessary, and we would do our best to provide them. 'If you do not ask it will be your fault. If you do ask and do not get what you need it will be ours.' I said the Cabinet expected 'Jerusalem before Christmas'.[1]

The Prime Minister's emphatic tone gives the misleading impression that he was in charge of his generals, and that his plans for the Palestine campaign were well thought-out and only needed implementation. In fact, civil-military relations in late 1917 were tense and problematic, and the differences between Lloyd George and Robertson reflected a lack of focused strategy by Britain, and impeded Allenby in his task out in Palestine.

With the coming to power of Lloyd George in December 1916, and his introduction of a leaner War Cabinet, civil-military relations entered a difficult phase. How best to direct the war had been a point of contention under the previous Prime Minister, Herbert Asquith, but with Lloyd George as leader matters came to a head.[2] If Lloyd George's remark about capturing Jerusalem for Christmas is taken uncritically, the conclusion is that Allenby's task was straightforward, not complicated by any behind-the-scenes differences and difficulties. But the South African general, Jan Smuts, who was offered the command of the EEF over Allenby, turned it down precisely because he knew that the military and the War Office were

Dr Matthew Hughes is a lecturer in modern history at Nene College, Northampton.

David Lloyd George, 14 May 1918. Q 72740

not fully behind the operation, preferring to focus attention on the main fighting in France.[3] Because of Allenby's perceived failure with Third Army at the battle of Arras in April 1917 he did not have Smuts's option, and he was angry at being moved from France to Palestine.[4]

The usual description of the contrast between Lloyd George and the 'generals' are the over-worked and rather simplistic terms 'easterners' versus 'westerners'. There was a divergence of opinion between those such as Robertson and Field Marshal Sir Douglas Haig who wanted to concentrate all efforts on the main front in France, and politicians such as Lloyd George who sought victory by reinforcing outlying war zones. However, simply to heap policy-makers into one or other category is misleading. Those at the centre of power such as Lloyd George and Robertson were astute, and able to see the complexities surrounding prosecution of the Great War. Certainly where Robertson was concerned, his affected exterior of a man who had risen through the ranks and dropped his aitches belied an accomplished linguist and a sharp mind.[5]

The 'westerner' Robertson was also an 'easterner' inasmuch as he was keenly aware of the need to protect the British Empire's eastern possessions: more so as with Russia's collapse in 1917 there was a power vacuum in the Caucasus region. Lloyd George was a 'westerner' in that as far as he understood military questions, he realised that Germany had to be defeated on the Western Front.

The difference was more subtle than 'easterner' and 'westerner'. The Prime Minister was aware of the need to preserve British power for use during and after the fighting. What he wanted was to shift the burden of the fighting onto the shoulders of others such as the French, or Americans, and in doing so save Britain's power as represented by her armed forces. Robertson felt that his task was to keep war policy on course and out of the hands of military amateurs like Lloyd George. It was not so much 'easterners' and 'westerners', as 'long-term' versus 'short-term' strategists. It was not that Lloyd George thought that he could win the war in Palestine, more that he became increasingly convinced that Haig would lose it in France with costly offensives like the Battle of Passchendaele. Robertson's fear was that in pursuance of his 'long-term' strategy Lloyd George would lose the war.

Robertson was conscious of the worrying implications of Russia's collapse for the British Empire in the East.[6] But he saw little military value in pursuing campaigns such as the EEF's in Palestine. He saw them as a waste of time, energy and resources, and was content to deal with military threats such as the Central Powers' push towards Baku on the Caspian Sea with small, specialist military missions.[7] In his autobiography, published in 1921, Robertson complained that at least 20 per cent of the time of the General Staff in 1917 was spent assessing peripheral operations.[8] If Robertson's figure is accurate, it is indicative of Lloyd George's attempt to promote operations in regions such as the Levant.

Lloyd George, who had never been on active service, viewed the Palestine campaign as a way of somehow preventing the costly offensives in France.[9] This seems to have been the main reason for his promoting it. He also hoped that by 'knocking away the props' of German allies such as Turkey, a Middle East campaign would cause Germany herself to collapse. This, however, ignored the real state of affairs: it was Germany which propped up the Ottoman empire and not *vice versa*. The idea of 'knocking away the props' was more a justification *post facto* put forward by those such as Sir Maurice Hankey, head of the War Cabinet secretariat, as a reason for the Palestine campaign. In 1917 the motivation behind the campaign was an indirect one aiming to prevent renewed Passchendaele-style offensives in France. Lloyd George was also keenly aware of the need to provide Britain with territorial bargaining counters for any post-war peace settlement, and Palestine and Syria could supply these.

However this strategy disregarded both the pressing needs of the war and the fact that if Britain were to lose in France, occupation of parts of the Middle East would count for little in any post-war negotiations. Robertson and the General Staff were concerned about the German troops which following the Russian Revolution were being railed west, and which would be used in the five Ludendorff offensives of 1918.[10]

In his memoirs Robertson wrote how: 'the advance into Palestine had for its main object the thwarting of hostile designs against Mesopotamia, and not the capture of Jerusalem'.[11] This parochial operational view can be contrasted with a speech given by the Prime Minister to Parliament on 20 December 1917 following Jerusalem's capture:

> The British Empire owes a great deal to side-shows. During the Seven Years' War . . . the events which are best remembered by every Englishman are not the great battles on the continent of Europe, but Plassey and the Heights of Abraham; and I have no doubt at all that, when the history of 1917 comes to be written, and comes to be read ages hence, these events in Mesopotamia and Palestine will hold a much more conspicuous place in the minds and the memories of people than many an event which looms much larger for the moment in our sight.[12]

Lloyd George and Robertson, while seemingly at variance, were looking at two sides of the same coin. Both wanted to defeat Germany. Yet while Robertson kept his focus firmly on the military, Lloyd George's purview was very much the wider political and imperial dimension. These different approaches need not have been, and should not have been, mutually exclusive.

Criticism of Lloyd George should be measured against the propaganda value of successes in peripheral war zones. For a national war effort a feat such as Jerusalem's capture was a propaganda *coup*. Lloyd George certainly made the most of it, announcing the event first in the House of Commons, with the whole affair 'carefully stage-managed'.[13] The London *Islington Daily Gazette* recorded how: 'By the capture of Jerusalem, General Allenby has made his Palestine campaign historic. More than military significance attaches to the surrender into British hands of a city held in reverence by all Christendom.' The *Gazette* then noted what the Germans had to say in their Cologne *Volkszeitung*: 'This is doubtless a success for the English, though more moral than military . . . the conqueror of the city, of course, gains a halo.'[14] These comments from a small local paper show the value of Allenby's success. The media impact of Jerusalem's fall was lessened by the Lansdowne letter on 29 November 1917, and then by a huge explosion in Halifax harbour in Canada in early December 1917, but these were not events that Lloyd George could have prepared for. The boost to national morale resulting from the occupation of Palestine should not be underestimated, especially as in December 1917 the outlook for Britain was bleak.

In late 1917 it looked as if the war would continue beyond 1918 into 1919, or even 1920. For the Entente, 1917 was very much the year of 'strain' with Russia's collapse, Italy's defeat at Caporetto, mutinies in the French army following the Nivelle offensive, unrestricted submarine warfare, and the slowness of the build-up of American troops. Talking to Hankey in

Field Marshal Sir William Robertson, 26 July 1917. Q 58590

October 1917, Lloyd George outlined his worries saying Britain should save herself for 'the great and terrible effort in 1919'.[15] By the time of this conversation Britain had been fighting for over three years, and the situation was grim. In a letter to Lord Murray in July 1917, Lord Esher wrote: 'Both in England and France, men are old and weary. Even those young in years are too travelled-stained to make any show.'[16] The war seemed interminable, and if 1917 managed to be worse than 1916, the fear was, what would 1918 bring?[17] The spring and summer of 1917 saw industrial disputes in Britain, and this, coupled with the rise of the Bolsheviks in Russia, made those in power alarmed by the threat of nascent revolutionary movements.[18]

In this context Britain's prosecution of the war was crucial. With the capture of Messines Ridge in June 1917, the stage was set for Field Marshal Douglas Haig's offensive towards Passchendaele. Lloyd George was very bitter about the casualties incurred at third Ypres, and the Prime Minister's anger was reflected in his relationship with Robertson. In 1932, talking to the military thinker Basil Liddell Hart, Lloyd George remarked: 'Haig utterly stupid. That was the man we made an earl. And I gave £100,000 to.'[19] The Prime Minister felt that Robertson blindly backed Haig: 'Robertson never attempted to guide strategy of [the] war. Merely backed Haig and would have backed a successor similarly.'[20]

There is some substance in the idea that Robertson did agree with Haig, but a more accurate assessment would be that Robertson 'believed that he had no choice but to support Haig. If he did not, he feared that the civilians would exploit the disunity within the high command to redirect higher strategy.'[21] Lloyd George's post-war anger towards Robertson and the 'generals' should not detract from the broad correctness of Robertson's continual attempts to point out to his political master the relative military importance of France as compared with Palestine. That Robertson did not agree with Lloyd George's Palestine campaign did not mean, *ipso facto*, that the CIGS had no strategy of his own.

Lloyd George's enthusiasm for Allenby to push on stood in marked contrast to the CIGS's pessimism. Robertson remarked to Haig how Lloyd George was 'very keen on capturing Jerusalem and this of course I...had to fight and I intend continuing to do so...But it is very disturbing all the same to have these hankerings after other plans and mistrust in present ones.'[22]

The civil-military dispute served to make Allenby's job harder, and it was an unnecessary distraction at a pivotal time for Britain in the First World War. When the Eastern expert Sir Mark Sykes returned to London in mid-September 1917 'the War Cabinet still had not agreed on how far Allenby should go in Palestine'.[23] During the meeting of the Cabinet Committee on War Policy of 3 October 1917 Smuts pointed out that current instructions to Allenby: 'did not mean the conquest of Palestine which indicated that we had not settled a policy at present for knocking out the Turks.'[24] As Allenby was to begin the third battle of Gaza by assaulting Beersheba in southern Palestine on 30 October, it is difficult to locate his assault in a clear central strategic framework.

Neither can clarity in the direction of the war be found in the international conferences Britain held with France. The two conferences of 25-26 July and 7-8 August 1917 succeeded in allowing one division—the 10th (Irish)—to be moved from Salonika to Palestine.[25] Yet this was a hard-won victory for Lloyd George, and not until the London conference in August was it finally agreed actually to move the division to Egypt. As Hankey pointed out: 'The whole morning was spent in discussing and wrangling over a ridiculous question of moving one division from Salonika to Egypt', the whole affair being 'very futile'.[26]

The complications of alliance warfare adversely affected war policy which was further handicapped by the problems of co-ordinating the campaigns in Salonika and Palestine. Britain had no intention of allowing France a role of any importance in Palestine in military terms, knowing that France would use her assistance as a bargaining counter after the war. France, likewise, did not want Britain to land at Alexandretta, behind the Turkish lines, as she considered this area in her imperial 'zone'. The Zionist, Chaim Weizmann, in June 1917, told W Ormsby Gore that 'the French policy in Greece was partly dictated by the desire to prevent our reinforcing the Palestinian front so as to prevent Britain gaining a footing in Palestine.'[27] France preferred the British troops to remain at Salonika where they did little and suffered badly from malaria.

The Cabinet Committee on War Policy was one of the many committees spawned by the War Cabinet. The twenty one meetings held by the committee in 1917 illustrate many of the damaging effects of the civil-military dispute in late 1917 on war strategy.[28] Reading the minutes is to discover a depressing catalogue of prevarication and indecision: 'a talking shop, seldom sticking to its agenda and almost never reaching positive conclusions which could be passed by the secretariat to the appropriate department for action.'[29] The final meeting on 11 October 1917 (possibly misdated and held on the 9th[30]) witnessed Lord Milner replying to advice given by Major-General Lynden-Bell in the previous meeting. Lynden-Bell (ex-Chief of General Staff, EEF) was seen as Robertson's representative, and the following comment by Milner captures some of the spirit of civil-military relations:

> Lord Milner said he was quite undiscouraged by General Lynden-Bell's evidence [against attacking Turkey]. If Sir Douglas Haig had approached his problem in the same spirit, he could have made an even stronger case against doing no more. In fact, the military made no proposals. They waited for the War Cabinet to make proposals, and then they overthrew them.[31]

Lloyd George backed Milner by pointing out that Lynden-Bell 'when asked if the whole resources of the British Empire were put at his disposal could he smash the Turks, he had replied in the negative'.[32] These deliberations were not conclusive, and the debate over whether to attack Turkey through Palestine carried on into 1918.

In an attempt to give himself military credibility, Lloyd George used Lord French (ex-Commander-in-Chief of the army in France) to prepare a report that was submitted on 20 October 1917.[33] General Sir Henry Wilson also helped with this report that was critical of first Haig, and then Robertson. In French's report Robertson's negative attitude to the Palestine campaign received the retort:

> To my mind the idea of staking the remainder of our resources on one desperate blow after another on the Western Front has become much more of a 'gamble' than anything else we have undertaken in this war. This method has been given a very long and patient trial under the most favourable conditions.[34]

Lord French continued that in his opinion an offensive in Palestine: 'offered such favourable chances and possibilities as should have induced the General Staff to bring it up for discussion by the War Cabinet at a time when it would have been possible to consider it'.[35] This is important, as what French saw as a feasible military operation was now impracticable due to the lateness of any attack. This, said French, meant that the possibility that the spring of 1918 could have seen Turkey out of the war, would now not be realised. Because the Palestine campaign had been delayed by those such as Robertson, French felt that 'it would be impossible to look for any decisive action by an army operating in that theatre [Palestine] before the winter of 1918'.[36]

If French is correct, the military had succeeded in their task of keeping the focus of the war in France. The idea that the military command was unable to see and act on Lloyd George's strategical insight is reinforced. However, a closer examination of the Palestine campaign shows serious flaws in Lloyd George's plan for a victory there. Robertson, and the General Staff, were perfectly correct, as military experts, to be sceptical about the Palestine offensive. The triumvirate of Enver, Talaat and Djemal Pasha who effectively ruled the Ottoman empire became uninterested in Palestine, preferring to pursue expansionist aims in the Caucasus.[37] The Turks looked to link up with fellow 'Turanian' speakers in Asia, and the loss to them of part of Syria or Palestine would have been bearable. More than this, in what fashion would the occupation of, say, Damascus defeat Turkey? The one operation that could have removed the Ottoman Empire from the war was the assault at Gallipoli in 1915. Short of Allenby marching the EEF across the Anatolian heartland and threatening Istanbul, Turkey was going to stay in the war.

That a drive to Aleppo — some 350 miles from Jerusalem — would not endanger the core of Ottoman economic and political activity which was based around Istanbul was pointed out in papers by British military representatives within the Supreme War Council (SWC), but seems not to have influenced the plans of Lloyd George: 'The loss of DAMASCUS or ALEPPO would have a serious moral effect on the Turks, but neither of these places nor MOSUL are, strategically speaking, of very great importance to the cause of the Central Powers'. The military representatives went on to observe that:

General Sir Edmund Allenby. Q 82969

> In Palestine no definite or adequate objective offers itself. Even if it were possible to seize ALEPPO it would not be worthwhile to use up any considerable resources for the importance of the place has dwindled to comparatively small proportions in consequence of the new lines of communication now available for the Turkish Army by the Black Sea to Caucasia.[38]

The accuracy of these military reports was borne out in September-October 1918 when the Ottomans sued for peace. They did so following the surrender of Bulgaria, which cut Turkey's land link to Germany, who herself was retreating in France. Turkey was well aware of her reliance on Germany as the strongest power in her alliance.

In September-October 1918, following the Battle of Megiddo, the EEF did advance to Aleppo, but this was not what caused the Turks to surrender on 30 October 1918. The Allied army at Salonika had attacked on 15 September, and the Central Powers' front quickly collapsed. This was more threatening to Istanbul than Allenby's attack in Palestine. In turn, the Central Powers' collapse in Salonika and Palestine related very much to the retreat of the German army in France from August 1918.

A fair conclusion would be that both Robertson and Lloyd George were 'right'. They had, however, different conceptions of the war. The CIGS saw the military dimension and the need to fight the 'amateurs', as represented by those like the Prime Minister. This was in contrast to Lloyd George and his far wider political brief to deal with the morale of the home front; to give Britain something to bargain with after the war which would help to keep the empire intact; to keep his own coalition government in power; and in general to see matters in a way that some of the military experts were unable to because of the more specific nature of their work.[39]

With Jerusalem's capture Lloyd George did get his Christmas present for the nation, and he was acutely aware not only of its value for home front morale, but of the negative attitude of the War Office to 'this historic triumph'.[40] But if a case can be made for Lloyd George's pursuit of the Palestine campaign up to December 1917, his continued attempts—one might even say obsession—to force through more action in Palestine after December 1917 are harder to comprehend.

The General Staff repeatedly told Lloyd George that a German offensive in the West was impending. As has been mentioned the Palestine campaign was highly unlikely to force Turkey out of the war. These two factors, coupled with the fact that there were no cities with the sentimental attachment of Jerusalem for Allenby to capture after December 1917, support Robertson's stance.

Cities such as Beirut, Damascus, Homs, Hama or Aleppo had none of the religious significance of Jerusalem. Indeed, one suspects most ordinary British people would not have known of these places. Jerusalem was a different matter in an era where people had a far more detailed grasp of the Bible, and Allenby's success was very much portrayed as a reversal of the defeat of 1187 when Saladin recaptured the city from the Crusaders.

It is appropriate here to examine the charge made by Lloyd George (and after the war by those like Leopold Amery, Liddell Hart, and more recently, David Woodward) that Robertson and Allenby colluded to deceive the Prime Minister. This was a serious accusation in itself, but even more serious in late 1917 with the implication that Lloyd George's Palestine campaign was maliciously thwarted.

Military duplicity towards Lloyd George

Following a conversation with Lloyd George after the war Liddell Hart noted that: 'L[loyd] G[eorge] remarked that he had never known politicians tell a deliberate lie. "They colour, exaggerate, but they avoid a lie because of the heavy risk of being tripped up". G[eneral] S[taff] told L G *palpable lies*.'[41]

The aim in this article is to show that Robertson and Allenby were faithful in the reports they gave. But Lloyd George's conviction that he was not being told the truth led him to disregard the advice given to him by his military experts concerning the Palestine campaign. This was a serious matter as Lloyd George was doing away with the military advice which was essential for a unified war effort with the 'frocks' and the 'brasshats' working together.

An assessment Allenby made which reached the War Cabinet on 10 October 1917 is the most egregious example of a military report designed to stop the Palestine offensive. David Woodward has described it as 'one of the most absurd appreciations ever presented to a British government'.[42] In his report to Robertson on 9 October 1917 Allenby pointed out that he would need a total of twenty three divisions to capture Jerusalem and hold southern Palestine. He was asking for an extra thirteen infantry divisions (in addition to the seven infantry and three cavalry divisions he already commanded).

Considering that Allenby went on in November-December 1917 at the Third Battle of Gaza to capture and hold Jerusalem with his existing ten divisions, one sees the incongruity of his assessment. The War Cabinet in December 1917 was not slow to point out to Robertson the curious nature of the October request.[43]

David Woodward describes Robertson's actions as 'cooking' the figures to force Lloyd George to act cautiously, and that Robertson did so by sending Allenby a secret 'R' telegram to get him to make this inflated estimate of twenty-three divisions. But the telegram in which Robertson asked Allenby for his report on future plans and requirements for Palestine is straightforward. To see a conspiracy in Robertson's correspondence with Allenby is to transform reasoned reports into something sinister.[44] If Allenby's October report were part of a 'plot' why, on 9 October, did Robertson assess Allenby's divisional requirements as an extra five divisions, leaving Allenby's more inflated estimate of the same day looking rather forlorn?[45]

Robertson was simply reacting to a genuine report by Allenby. While Robertson needed little prompting to do this, as Allenby's divisional assessment supported his own view that a Palestine offensive was problematic, this did not mean that Robertson was acting in bad faith. The fairest conclusion is that Allenby genuinely misread Turkish capabilities and intentions. It should be remembered that Allenby had supposedly failed at the Battle of Arras, and he could not sustain another defeat and keep command: this led him to act methodically.

British intelligence on the Turks was faulty and served the exaggerated view of a possible Turkish offensive in Palestine. The fear of a potential Turkish attack in Palestine, coupled with the need to garrison occupied areas, was the foundation for Allenby's request for twenty-three divisions. The water problem surrounding the impending Third Battle of Gaza compounded Allenby's concerns. The Third Battle of Gaza relied for success on Allenby's Australian mounted infantry capturing the wells at Beersheba intact. Luckily, as the German demolition officer stationed in Beersheba was on leave, only two of Beersheba's seventeen wells were blown up as the Australians charged in on 31 October 1917.[46] But Allenby's fear was of his troops being left out on a limb because of the lack of water.

The Turks were, indeed, planning an offensive in Palestine. They were putting together a force, usually called *Yilderim*, meaning 'thunderbolt' or 'lightning' after the Ottoman ruler, Bâyezîd (c.1360–1402), though by the Germans it was more normally referred to as *Heeresgruppe F*.[47] While British intelligence reports indicated that up to four German divisions were destined for Palestine, the reality was that the *Yilderim* force contained only three German infantry battalions. This nucleus was added to an existing German force of artillery and technical units called 'Pasha I', and was itself reinforced by four further battalions, but none of these German units arrived in time for the third battle of Gaza.[48] In fact, the force was something of a chimera.

The reality by late 1917 was that no small specialist force, however competent, would be able to make up for the general deficiencies of the Ottoman empire. The Turkish pledge of nine divisions for *Yilderim* indicated that it was a force to be taken seriously. However, of these nine divisions only two (the 19th and 24th) arrived in time to take part in the third battle of Gaza. The 20th Division arrived at the front before Jerusalem's fall, and two divisions were broken up *en route*. As for the remaining four divisions, they arrived fitfully and in a much depleted condition.[49] The state of the Turkish railway system, coupled with national war-weariness, made any Turkish division that arrived in Palestine very much a nominal formation.[50]

The British misread the capabilities and intentions of the Ottomans. Turkish troops released by the collapse of Russia were used in a gradual drive on Baku: they were not sent to Palestine. Baku did not fall until September 1918, and the *Yilderim* force was not the threat it seemed. This was the real background to the accusation that the 'generals' 'lied' to Lloyd George.

Camel transport of the Desert Mounted Corps on the march in the Judean Hills. Q 12707

General Allenby's official entry into Jerusalem, 11 December 1917. Q 12616

The problem with the Palestine campaign in late 1917 was a profound one. War strategy was in turmoil at the time, and this was not due to the General Staff acting in bad faith. The malaise lay deeper. In a comparison to Winston Churchill and the Second World War, Malcolm Thomson in his biography of Lloyd George gets some way towards the truth, writing that: 'Lloyd George never possessed such authority [as Churchill]; and in consequence the year 1917 was a period of frustration for him as regards its military operations.'[51] The real difficulty for Lloyd George was that he could not direct matters as he might have wished. In the last resort he did not know enough to be truly sure of himself. It is also worth noting, *en passant*, that Churchill's 'direction' of the war did, on occasion, cause his military advisers some problems as the Prime Minister pursued various impossible schemes to defeat Germany.

As to Allenby's complicity in any military 'plot' to trick Lloyd George, the evidence shows Allenby to have been honest in his dealings. He made his request for twenty-three divisions fairly soon after arriving in Palestine, and this estimate should be viewed within the context of a new commander getting to grips with his new force. To emphasise Allenby's request is to ignore that commanders of armies usually ask for more than is absolutely necessary. Allenby was not unique in trying to get as many men as possible to deal with the vagaries of war.

The charge that Robertson was deliberately lying was a very serious one, and Lord Derby (Secretary of State for War) writing to Lloyd George, felt the accusation 'almost beyond belief', as Robertson was essentially 'honest'.[52] Arthur Balfour, the Foreign Secretary, was perhaps closest to the truth when he wrote to Andrew Bonar Law that as the military were not behind a Palestine campaign little would happen. This was not to say they acted in a deceitful fashion, more that they were simply lack-lustre in their attitude to a renewed eastern offensive.[53] As has been shown they had reasons for being this way.

The Palestine Campaign, December 1917 to October 1918

After the fall of Jerusalem on 9 December 1917 the civil-military dispute surrounding the Palestine campaign continued. The culmination of the dispute between Lloyd George and Robertson came on 1 February 1918 when the Supreme War Council accepted Joint Note 12 that proposed a decisive offensive effort against Turkey, with a defensive role to be adopted in France.[54] General Jan Smuts was then sent on a mission to Egypt, and on 1 March 1918 he submitted his report on how Allenby's campaign should be pursued to put into effect the conclusion of Joint Note 12.

From before Jerusalem's fall, Lloyd George kept up the pressure on the CIGS so that the momentum of the Palestine offensive would not be lost. Via Robertson, Lloyd George put ever increasing pressure on Allenby. The capture of Jerusalem only served to excite further the Prime Minister's hopes for a decisive offensive in Palestine. Rather than see the capture of Jerusalem as the successful outcome of a limited offensive with a specific objective, the Prime Minister viewed Allenby's victory at Jerusalem as part of an ongoing campaign.

From 12 December, the day after Allenby triumphantly walked through the Jaffa Gate into Jerusalem, the Prime Minister began the pressure that was to culminate in Joint Note 12.[55] On 12 December Robertson wrote to Allenby that: 'the War Cabinet would like to have your opinion...as soon as possible as to manner in which, and extent to which, it is possible to exploit your success in Palestine with forces now under your command'.[56]

Replying on the 14th, Allenby gave a watchful assessment, seeing little possibility of any substantial advance before the summer of 1918. He saw the restrictive effects of the winter rains, and proposed a gradual advance based on double-tracking his railway and pushing it up the coast. He also hoped to operate against the Hedjaz railway supplying Medina, an operation for which he was partly to rely on the military assistance of his Arab ally.

However, this reasoned assessment was not sufficient for the War Cabinet, and the CIGS had again to telegraph Allenby on the 18th to tell him that his political masters attached 'great importance to eliminating Turkey' and, therefore, wanted a project to deal with two possibilities: firstly, the occupation of Palestine as far north as Mount Hermon; secondly, an advance to Aleppo and interdiction of the Turks' supply route to Mesopotamia.[57]

This request prompted Allenby to reply on 20 December that he would need 16 to 18 divisions besides his three mounted divisions.[58] This request, however, was for an advance to the line Damascus-Beirut and beyond. Considering that Turkey in late 1917 was still in the war, and being supported by Germany, Allenby's assessment was thoughtful, reasoned, and not fanciful. Also, Allenby said that to occupy only Palestine was something he could do by the summer with his existing force if Turkish opposition was under 60,000. When Allenby said to the CIGS that Aleppo was some 350 miles from his railhead, and its occupation no easy task, this was a reasonable comment, and not an example of his being deliberately misleading.

One needs to ask what might have happened to the EEF forward units if they had advanced to Aleppo. They would have been confronted by Turkish forces weakened, but not at all defeated, and with Germany still as an ally. The Turks would also have benefited from a shortened logistical train. General Marshall's force in Mesopotamia would have been unable to provide much help as it would have been denuded of troops to reinforce the EEF.[59] Indeed, if Smuts's plans, as embodied in his report of March 1918, had gone ahead the Mesopotamian force would have been left with only four infantry divisions.[60]

In October 1918, when the cavalry of Allenby's 5th Indian Division did finally occupy Aleppo, they did so only with difficulty, and they were the only cavalry unit able to make the long march north from Damascus, as the other three cavalry divisions were too debilitated by malaria.[61] They were also facing an enemy weakened by the long summer, and the drain of the Caucasian offensive that culminated in Baku's capture by the Turks in September 1918.[62] Regarding malaria, the anopheline species of mosquito that causes malaria would have been most prevalent in the summer of 1918 following the rainy season[63]—and the Turks' lack of prophylactic measures meant that malaria was rife behind their lines. If the EEF had pushed deep into Turkish territory in early 1918, the troops would have been badly affected by endemic malaria.

In late 1918 the conditions behind the Turkish lines led to famine in Lebanon and Syria. The sufferings of the civilians would have been another problem for which the EEF would have had to direct resources. These factors made the calculation of the number of troops that Allenby would need for any occupation of Palestine, Syria and Lebanon very difficult.

Had Allenby succeeded in advancing into northern Syria in early 1918, and then had lost his trained infantry force to Haig in France to deal with the Ludendorff offensives, which was precisely what did happen, the EEF might have had to retreat. This would have had an adverse effect on home front morale, precisely when the British and French armies were themselves retreating in France. In considering whether Robertson and Allenby misled Lloyd George, these difficulties must be taken into account. While there would certainly be advantages that would accrue to Britain by Allenby's successes, Britain had limits to her resources and, unfortunately for her, could not do everything that she wished.

If Allenby had had more rapid success at the Third Battle of Gaza, and linked this to an aggressive policy from late 1917 with a correct assessment of Turkish capabilities and intentions, Palestine, and possibly parts of Syria, might have been occupied before September 1918.

However, whether the value of this occupation would have outweighed the damage caused by the drain on resources is debatable. The occupation of the whole of Syria, which is what Lloyd George wanted, would have involved the EEF in a long-term military commitment. If Turkey had stayed in the war, Robertson's assessment of the number of troops that would have been needed to confront the Turks in northern Syria was more accurate. After the armistice in October 1918, large numbers of British troops had to be maintained in Syria, and if the British had occupied Syria before the total collapse of Turkey, many soldiers would have been needed for internal policing.[64]

For instance, during the drive on Damascus in September 1918, Sir Harry Chauvel, the commander of Allenby's cavalry corps, had to despatch four cavalry regiments to keep order around Kuneitra on the Golan Heights because of the hostility of the local inhabitants who were largely Circassian and pro-Ottoman.[65] The endemic disorder of the region had forced the Ottomans to maintain large garrisons before the war. For their punitive expedition into the Hauran mountains in Syria in 1910, the Turks had deployed 21,000 soldiers, with limited success at cowing the inhabitants into submission.[66] Britain would undoubtedly have had to deploy substantial forces in the area just to maintain order.

Since the assumption in London in 1918 was that the Great War would continue into 1919, any analysis of British war policy must ask whether a prolonged garrisoning of Lebanon and Syria would have been a wise use of scarce resources. In July 1918 the War Office was insisting that any reinforcements which Allenby might receive would have to be returned for the campaign in France in the spring of 1919.[67] The war ended in November 1918, but this was not foreseen.

It is not even apparent that if the EEF had occupied Aleppo they would have succeeded in completely cutting off the Turkish Sixth Army in Mesopotamia. In Smuts's report of 1 March 1918 he asserted that any advance from Mesopotamia would have its right flank threatened from the north. This was one of the reasons that led Smuts to conclude that an offensive in Palestine, as opposed to Mesopotamia, would have more effect. This may be, but if so it makes his subsequent assertion that an advance to Aleppo would isolate the Turks in Mesopotamia inconsistent.[68] If the Turks were able to threaten from eastern Asia Minor they were also presumably equally able to supply their Mesopotamian force from that area of Turkey evacuated by the Russian army after the Russian Revolution. Thus an advance to Aleppo would not necessarily have detached the Turkish Sixth Army in northern Mesopotamia, and Marshall would only have had four infantry divisions to maintain pressure from the east.

In September 1918, with the Central Powers in retreat, the EEF was able to deal a decisive blow to the Turks in Palestine at the Battle of Megiddo, and install Prince Feisal and his Northern Arab Army in Damascus. However, whether this would have been possible, or desirable, earlier in 1918 is not so obvious. Lloyd George did not seem to see all the military implications of the Palestine campaign to the wider war as he moved his dispute with his CIGS to the Supreme War Council.

Lloyd George's view was that the General Staff were telling him 'palpable lies'.[69] Whether true or not, the Prime Minister seemed to believe this charge. Thus he ended up disregarding Robertson, and on 21 January 1918 the military representatives of the Supreme War Council submitted Joint Note 12, which Lloyd George seized on as a means to undo the CIGS.[70]

This note was agreed on at the third meeting of the Supreme War Council, 30 January–2 February 1918, but Lloyd George's strength of feeling is shown by the fact that before then the War Cabinet on 28 January ordered Smuts on his mission to decide whether the offensive should be in Palestine—and, if so, what reinforcements would be needed.[71] Lloyd George was obviously determined to push through an eastern strategy, and the records of the third meeting of the Supreme War Council amply show this.[72] Even Georges Clemenceau, the French premier, said that they should take into account Robertson's reservations, but Lloyd George was adamant, and put aside Robertson's fears that to attempt Joint Note 12 would be 'very dangerous'.[73]

For Robertson and the General Staff the difficulty with Joint Note 12 was that part which dealt with the safety of Britain and the maintenance of the front in France. Both Robertson and the General Staff were explicit about the value of keeping up the pressure on the Turks and, if possible, forcing them from the war. However, from before the conference that accepted Joint Note 12, Robertson and the military were drawing attention to the importance of the front in France, and how the Note was complacent concerning the impending German offensive.[74] Strong support for Robertson's view is provided by the fact that most of Allenby's force had to return to France once the Ludendorff offensives were launched on 21 March 1918.

The main problem was whether the British army in France was under strength, a disagreement that culminated with the 'Maurice letter' in May 1918.[75] The disagreement with Major-General Frederick Maurice, the Director of Military Operations, in May 1918 also raises the question of whether Lloyd George himself was not above a bit of 'lying' when it suited him.[76] There is not the space here to deal with the question of whether the British Expeditionary Force in France had enough men to deal with the Germans, but in relation to the Palestine campaign, was Lloyd George's strategy militarily the most expedient one? To assert, as Lloyd George did, that Germany had gained many advantages from her eastern strategy is probably true. What does not follow, and ignores differences like Germany's centripetal communication network, is that Britain could achieve the same.[77]

General Jan Smuts went out to Egypt, 12–22 February, to organise a plan of action to implement Lloyd George's wishes.[78] Colonel Richard Meinertzhagen, an EEF staff officer, wrote in his diary: 'It is curious that we should have to rely on a Dutchman for advice which could be given by either the War Office or Allenby'.[79] Lloyd George was using Smuts as his 'trouble-shooter' because he was tired of hearing the assessments of the military. Smuts, who had come round to his way of thinking, was the right choice for Lloyd George.[80] Sir Walter Kirke, who went on Smuts's Mission, commented that Smuts's job was: 'to lend his bogus but considerable military prestige to supporting anything proposed by Lloyd George'.[81] Amery's comment on Joint Note 12 that Wilson is 'pushing along at top speed,

The first batch of prisoners taken by 7th Indian Division at the Battle of Megiddo, 19 September 1918. Q 12972

and the result ought to be a document on which you can then act without hesitation and in the face of any obstruction'[82] does point to Lloyd George's determination to override Robertson's objections.

Smuts submitted his report on how best to implement the ideas embodied in Joint Note 12 on 1 March 1918.[83] In three weeks' time the first German offensive commenced against the British Third and Fifth Armies, so what Smuts had to say became irrelevant. Smuts's rather doctrinaire conclusions in his report meant that Allenby regarded him as a representative that he had to tolerate but would ignore if at all possible.

Smuts's first decision was that the impending offensive against the Ottoman Empire should come in Palestine, and not Mesopotamia, and for this Mesopotamia should send three divisions and some extra artillery, while France would provide an Indian cavalry division.[84] Leaving aside the strain on shipping, Smuts's proposals would have resulted in the EEF being augmented to ten infantry divisions, four mounted divisions, and a cavalry brigade, along with a strengthened artillery pool.

Once the gravity of the German offensives in France was realised, the EEF had to supply units to an extent that it was left with only one trained 'all-white' infantry division with twelve British battalions (the 54th), plus six divisions each with three trained British and nine untrained Indian battalions. This is a point worth emphasising in any analysis of war strategy. Because of the drain resulting from the Ludendorff offensive Allenby had to despatch 54 British battalions to France and replace them with an equal number of untrained Indian infantry battalions, as well as absorbing thirteen Indian cavalry squadrons. Allenby wrote to Wilson that 'the new arrivals are short of training', and added that some Pathans had deserted to the Turks.[85] The Ottoman Sultan was the spiritual leader for Sunni Muslims, and as 29 per cent of Allenby's newly arrived infantry were Muslims, this made Allenby's re-organisation particularly problematic. In July 1918 he cabled the War Office about his concern over unrest within his Indian drafts, and of the worrying presence of seditious documents written in 'Indian vernacular'.[86] If Allenby had attacked in the spring of 1918 he would have had to do so with the 54th Division: the only infantry division left to him intact.

Lloyd George claimed in his *War Memoirs* that Allenby's caution was: 'not due to any fear of being beaten by this miserable remnant of a defeated army, but rather to his dread of the consequences of brushing aside the restraining hand from Whitehall'.[87] This essay has attempted to show that the situation was more complicated than this in terms of the EEF's capabilities. Lloyd George continued by saying that the consequences of Allenby's inaction in early 1918 was that it 'enabled the Turks to hold out almost to the end, and to hold up hundreds of thousands of British troops'.[88] What can be added is that if the Prime Minister's strategy had been followed through by a vigorous and reinforced EEF earlier in the year, the outcome would probably have been precisely the same: Turkey still in the war, and Britain still with a substantial troop commitment in an area distant from the main fighting in France where the war was won.

Conclusion

That there were large British casualties on the Western Front did not mean that the calculations of Robertson and Allenby concerning Palestine were erroneous. With a German offensive impending, Britain simply did not have enough men to have both a 'western' and an 'eastern' strategy.

Robertson and the General Staff did push their case robustly, and the military, on occasion, were very narrow in their analysis of war strategy as it related to the campaigns in the Middle East. However, the argument that Lloyd George was the victim of military duplicity seems overstated. It has been argued here that Lloyd George's pursuit of a Palestine campaign after December 1917 was mistaken. This criticism of Lloyd George should be measured against the morale lifting capture of Jerusalem. Robertson's seeming inability to see merit in this success shows some of the CIGS's limitations. Criticism of Lloyd George in relation to the Palestine campaign should be set against his all-round effectiveness as a war leader.

In 1922, the year that David Lloyd George's coalition government fell from power, Herbert Asquith, the Liberal ex-Prime Minister sent Aubrey Herbert MP the following riddle: 'Question: What must a man do to bathe safely among sharks? Answer: Have tattooed on his back "Lloyd George won the war". No shark could swallow that.'[89] While amusing, Asquith's poser ignores Lloyd George's proficiency as Prime Minister during difficult years for Britain. His skills were the more noticeable when compared to Asquith's listless running of the war up to December 1916. For a national war effort a feat such as the capture of Jerusalem was a propaganda *coup* and Lloyd George made the most of it to try and lift spirits in Britain at a difficult time in the war.

Even with their differences, Lloyd George, Robertson, Haig, Allenby and the General Staff did present a formidable team that ultimately won the war. This does not necessarily excuse the time and energy wasted in late 1917 and in early 1918, but the retrospective certainty of hindsight must not obscure all the contingencies which Lloyd George, and Robertson, had to plan for.

Acknowledgement

I would like to thank the Trustees of the Liddell Hart Centre for Military Archives for permission to quote from material for which they have the copyright.

Abbreviations and Archives

Allenby hanging file: Middle East Centre, St. Antony's College, Oxford
Allenby papers: Liddell Hart Centre for Military Archives, King's College, London
AWM: Australian War Memorial, Canberra
Balfour papers: British Library
CAB: Cabinet papers at Public Record Office, Kew, London
CCWP: Cabinet Committee on War Policy
CIGS: Chief of the Imperial General Staff
Curzon papers: India Office Library, London
DLG: David Lloyd George
EEF: Egyptian Expeditionary Force
Esher papers: Churchill Archives Centre, Cambridge
Hankey papers: Churchill Archives Centre, Cambridge
Kirke papers: Imperial War Museum, London
LG: Lloyd George
LH: Liddell Hart
Liddell Hart papers: Liddell Hart Centre for Military Archives
Lloyd George papers: House of Lords Record Office
L/MIL: India Office, London
LSHTM: London School of Hygiene and Tropical Medicine
Meinertzhagen diaries: Rhodes House Library, Oxford
Milner papers: Bodleian Library, Oxford
Robertson papers: Liddell Hart Centre for Military Archives
SWC: Supreme War Council
Sykes papers: Brynmor Jones Library, Hull
WC: War Cabinet
WD: War Diary, Public Record Office, London
Wilson papers: Imperial War Museum London
WO: War Office, Public Record Office, London

Notes

1. Lloyd George, *War Memoirs*, vol ii, 1938, pp 1089-1090.
2. D Woodward, 'Britain in a Continental War: The Civil-Military Debate Over the Strategical Direction of the Great War of 1914-1918', *Albion*, Spring 1980, pp 37-65, shows how problems existed under Asquith, but that there was nothing like the acrimony between Lloyd George and elements of the military on direction of the war.
3. B Gardner, *Allenby*, 1965, p 111 and M Thomson, *David Lloyd George: The Official Biography*,1948, p 272. Smuts's correspondence re the appointment can be found in W K Hancock and J van der Poel, *Selections from the Smuts Papers*, vol iii, 1966, letters 741, 745, 757 & 762. My thanks to Dr M H van Meurs for checking the Smuts papers in Pretoria. See also Allenby hanging file, Jones to Wavell, 4 December 1936.
4. Allenby papers, 6/VIII/68, McMahon to Wavell, 18 October1936. Gardner, *Allenby*, p 113 says that Allenby was 'desolate' at having to go to Egypt.
5. Robertson's rise to the rank of field-marshal is told in Robertson, *From Private to Field Marshal*, 1921. See also David French, *Strategy of the Lloyd George Coalition*, 1985, for easterner vs westerner debate.
6. See for instance Robertson papers, I/17/1, 'Military Effect of Russia Seceding from the Entente', 9 May 1917 and I/17/3, 'The Present Military Situation in Russia and its Effect on our Future Plans', 29 July 1917.
7. Such as 'Dunsterforce', whose adventures are told by its commander in L Dunsterville, *The Adventures of Dunsterforce*, 1920. 'Dunsterforce' went through Persia and ultimately to Baku; for Trans-Caspia, Britain sent a force under General Malleson (see D Fromkin, *A Peace To End All Peace: Creating The Modern Middle East 1914–1922*,1991, pp 360–362).
8. Robertson, *From Private to Field Marshal*, p 319.
9. Lloyd George served in the militia for a short period, 1881–82 (see J Grigg, *The Young Lloyd George*, 1973, p 44).
10. Maurice Hankey (*The Supreme Command*, vol ii, 1961, pp 836–852) gives the impression the peripheral operations won the war. It would seem Robertson was right in discounting the military value of these side-shows. However, this ignores the political value of British forces in occupation of enemy territory.
11. Robertson, *From Private to Field Marshal*, pp 306–307.
12. P Guinn, *British Strategy and Politics 1914–1918*, 1965, footnote p 283 (from *Hansard*, col.2211, 20 December 1917 where Lloyd George greatly expands on the value of the Palestine campaign). Robertson saw little or no benefit in Jerusalem's capture saying, 'the military effect would be of no value to us.' (From Robertson papers, I/16/7/2c, 'Future Military Policy', 9 October 1917.)
13. J Newell, 'Learning The Hard Way: Allenby in Egypt and Palestine 1917–19', *Journal of Strategic Studies*, September 1991, p 372.
14. *Islington Daily Gazette & North London Tribune*, 12 December 1917 (Islington local history collection at central library).
15. Hankey papers, 8/2, 15 October 1917, 'Note by Sir Maurice Hankey of a Conversation between the Prime Minister and Himself', p 8 (copy also in CAB1/42). The WC on 30 October 1917 (meeting 259A) discussed whether to make the main Allied effort in 1918 or 1919. Wilson ('Memorandum by CIGS on possibility of war continuing to 1919', 19 March 1918) was emphatic (p 2) that war would go on into 1919 (CAB25/73).
16. Esher papers, journal 2/20, letter to Lord Murray, 28 July 1917.
17. J Turner, *British Politics and the Great War*, 1992, p 6. F Maurice, 'The Campaigns in Palestine and Egypt 1914–18 in relation to the General Strategy of the War', *The Army Quarterly*, April–July 1929, p 22 describes how Lloyd George wanted Palestine as a bargaining counter in a war which would go on until 1919.
18. Turner, *British Politics*, pp 5–7 and Guinn, *British Strategy*, p 235 and 242. Balfour papers, Add.Mss.49719, Esher to CIGS, 20 June 1917 for threat of revolution in Britain.
19. Liddell Hart papers, II/1932/42, 'Talk with Lloyd George—Generals in WW1', 24 September1932. Thomson, *DLG*, p 272 says Lloyd George 'never forgave Haig for Passchendaele'.
20. Ibid (LH papers).
21. D Woodward (ed), *The Military Correspondence of Field-Marshal Sir William Robertson*, 1989, p 194.
22. Robertson papers, I/23/40b, Robertson to Haig, 21 July 1917. D Woodward, 'Britain's "Brasshats" and the Question of a Compromise Peace 1916–18', *Military Affairs*, 1971, p 67, points to the new low in civil-military relations by late 1917.
23. M Adelson, *Mark Sykes: Portrait of an Amateur*, 1975, p 241.
24. 18th meeting of the Cabinet Committee on War Policy, 3 October 1917, p 2 (copies in Curzon papers, Mss Eur F112/136 and CAB27/6).
25. Minutes of the proceedings in Curzon papers (Allied Conference IC series), Mss Eur F112/152 (copies also in CAB28/2). See Hankey, *Supreme Command*, vol ii, pp 689–690 for August conference.
26. Hankey papers, diaries, 1/3 vol 2, 25–26 July 1917.
27. Sykes papers, DDSY(2)/12/8, report by Gore, 10 June 1917, p 3.
28. Of the 21 meetings numbers 15, 16, 18, 19, 20 and 21 dealt with Palestine. Various WP papers and reports were produced by the committee and copies can be found in CAB27/7–8 (also in Curzon papers, Mss Eur F112/135–136 and Milner papers V/B/360). There are no minutes for the 19th meeting as Hankey had a cold (see S Roskill, *Hankey: Man of Secrets*, 1970, vol i, p 440) although Robertson gives his side of what happened in WO106/721 (with Robertson saying not to attack in the east).
29. S Bidwell and D Graham, *Coalitions, Politicians and Generals: Some Aspects of Command in Two World Wars*, 1993, p 87.
30. See Woodward, *Lloyd George and the Generals* (footnote p 218) and *Military Correspondence of Field-Marshal Sir William Robertson* (footnote p 324).
31. CAB27/6, 21st meeting of CCWP, 11 October 1917, p 4.
32. Ibid.
33. CAB27/8, WP60, 'The Present State of the War, the Future Prospects, and Future Action to be taken. Memorandum prepared by Lord French in accordance with the request of the War Cabinet (WC247b, conclusion 7).' See also CAB23/

13/247(a), 10 October1917, pp 2–3 and 255(a), 23 October1917, pp 5–6 for WC views.

34. CAB27/8, report by French, p 16.

35. Ibid.

36. Ibid, p 23.

37. In fact the leadership of Turkey was more complicated than the usual idea of a clique of three: see F Ahmad, review of U Trumpener's *Germany and the Ottoman Empire 1914–18* in *Middle Eastern Studies*, January 1970, p 102.

38. CAB25/78, 'Probable enemy action in the Balkans and Turkey', Brigadier-General H Waters, GS, 22 July 1918, p 3 and CAB25/84, 'Proposed Joint Note', from British Military Representatives, 31 July 1918, p 5.

39. As B Busch describes it: 'The soldiers looked at maps of France; the amateurs looked at maps of the world.' (From *Britain, India and the Arabs*, 1971, p115.)

40. Lloyd George, *War Memoirs*, vol ii, 1938, p 1092.

41. Liddell Hart papers, II/1932/42, 'Talk with Lloyd George—Generals in WW1, LH's impressions of LG', 24 September1932 (my emphasis).

42. Woodward, *Lloyd George and the Generals*, 1983, p 206 and quoted in T Wilson, *The Myriad Faces of War*, 1986, p 500. For Allenby's report see Milner papers, V/B/360, W P 52, Robertson to Secretary War Cabinet, 10 October 1917 enclosing GOC-in-C GHQ Egypt to CIGS War Office, 9 October 1917.

43. See for instance Robertson defending the military to the War Cabinet in WO106/727, CIGS to War Cabinet, 14 December 1917 (also Cabinet minutes in CAB23/4/296(5), 12 December 1917). Robertson also brings up the subject of the Cabinet's annoyance in Robertson, *Soldiers and Statesmen*, vol ii, 1926, p 184.

44. Woodward, *Lloyd George and the Generals*, 1983, p 206 and p 231.

45. Robertson papers, I/16/7/2m, 'Occupation of Jaffa-Jerusalem Line', 9 October 1917. Robertson's letter to Hankey accompanying his report (I/16/7/1) gives the impression Robertson had little idea of Allenby's coming assessment (see also Robertson, *Soldiers and Statesmen*, vol ii, p 184).

46. P Dalbiac, *History of the 60th Division* (1927) p 123 for officer on leave. The Australian film *The Lighthorsemen* (1987) has an Australian Light Horse trooper dramatically (and presumably erroneously) saving the wells.

47. See CAB45/80, authors N-Y, H Pirie-Gordon to Becke, 4 April[?].

48. 'Notes on Foreign War Books', *The Army Quarterly*, July 1939, p 357. For *Yilderim* order of battle see C Falls and G Macmunn, *Military Operations: Egypt and Palestine*, HMSO 1928 and 1930, two volumes, vol ii, pp 42–43 and appendices 4, 5 and 6. (Hereafter known as *Official History*.) In fact Macmunn was not up to the job of writing the official history and Falls did all the work with Macmunn's name only appearing as a sop on vol i: CAB16/52/Paper 20, pp 7–8

49. For order of arrival see *Official History*, vol ii, p 24. See also C C R Murphy, 'The Turkish Army in the Great War', *RUSI Journal*, February 1920, p 103 and Hussein Husni Amir Bey, *Yilderim*, published by the Turkish General Staff. Translated by Capt. G O de R. Channer, (n.p. copy in 'Heyes papers' AWM 45[5/1]. Not bound, in a loose form).

50. For an overview of Turkey's railways see W Stanley, 'Review of Turkish Asiatic Railways to 1918: Some Political-Military Considerations', *The Journal of Transport History*, November 1966: published 1970, pp 189–203.

51. Thomson, *DLG*, p 270.

52. Lloyd George papers, F/14/4/83, Derby to PM, 11 December 1917.

53. Balfour papers, Add.Mss 49693, Balfour to B Law, 10 September 1917.

54. 'Joint Note 12 Submitted to the Supreme War Council by its Military Representatives', 21 January 1918. Copy in *History of the Great War, Belgium and France, 1918, Appendices*, 1935, appendix 9, para 19. Also in WO106/729 and CAB25/68 (by H Wilson dated 19 January 1918).

55. For November's correspondence see WO158/611, 16 and 17 November 1917; WO106/722, 'Resume of Operations in Palestine July 1917–April 1918', p 3 and Robertson papers, I/16/8a. For December's correspondence see CAB24/37, appendix to GT3112; WO33/946 and Robertson papers, I/16/9d.

56. 12 December 1917 telegram [also in CAB23/4/296(5)].

57. CAB24/37/GT3112, appendix, CIGS to Allenby, 18 December 1917, p 6.

58. Ibid, Allenby to CIGS, 20 December 1917, p 6.

59. If Smuts's proposals in February had gone ahead, two infantry divisions (including one British), one cavalry brigade (and a cavalry division from France) and artillery would have gone from the Mesopotamian force to the EEF (see *Official History*, vol ii, p 298).

60. Ibid and for Smuts's report see CAB24/4/G199, 'Report by General Smuts on his Mission to Egypt', 1 March 1918, p 3.

61. For casualties from malaria in 1918 see H S Gullett, *The Official History of Australia in the War of 1914–1918, Volume VII Sinai and Palestine, The Australian Imperial Force in Sinai and Palestine 1914–1918*, University of Queensland Press 1984, reprint of 1923 edition, pp 773, 780 and A J Hill, *Chauvel of the Light Horse*, 1978, p 183.

62. For Baku's fall see Fromkin, *A Peace To End All Peace*, pp 359–360 and Dunsterville, *The Adventures of Dunsterforce*, ch xvii.

63. See H S Leeson et al, 'Anopheles and Malaria in the Near East', *London School of Hygiene and Tropical Medicine, Memoir 7*, 1950, p 6. My thanks to Dr Chris Curtis and Ms Mary Gibson (at LSHTM) for their help in explaining malaria to me.

64. Circassians in the Trans-Jordan raids fired on the retreating EEF (WO95/4522, ANZAC Div, WD, 1 April 1918 and WO154/167, WD, May 1918, appendix 16), and were likewise hostile in the Golan Heights area later in 1918 (AWM25/455/9, 'Tactical Narrative. Australian Mounted Division. Operations Resulting in the Capture of Damascus', n.d., p 2). As part of their policy of backing Feisal the EEF troops, who universally seem to have despised Arabs (see for instance B Gammage, *The Broken Years*, 1974, pp 134–145), had to be told to be friendly to the local inhabitants.

65. *Official History*, vol ii, p 569.

66. C C R Murphy, *Soldiers of the Prophet*, 1921, p 13, pp 20–21.

67. WO33/960, WO to Allenby, 10 July 1918, p 19.

68. WO106/1545, G199, 'Report by General Smuts', 1 March 1918, pp 2–3 (copy also in CAB24/4).

69. Liddell Hart papers, II/1932/42, 'Talk with Lloyd George—Generals in WWI. LH's impressions of LG', 24 September1932.

70. Wilson at the SWC was asked to prepare Joint Note 12 on 31 December 1917 (see CAB25/43, Hankey to Wilson).

71. CAB23/5/332, WC minutes, 28 January 1918 (extract in WO106/729).

72. Record of the SWC meeting in CAB25/120 (also in Curzon papers, Mss Eur F112/153, IC40–41).

73. CAB25/120, SWC, third meeting, third session, pp 9–10.

74. WO106/729, CIGS (in France) to WO, 25 January 1918, pp 1–3 and ibid 'Comments by the General Staff upon Joint Note 12', 25 January 1918.

75. Ibid, p 2. See also D Woodward, 'Did Lloyd George Starve the British Army of Men Prior to the German Offensive of 21 March 1918?', *Historical Journal*, 27, 1(1984), pp 241–252.

76. That Lloyd George could be mischievous see Woodward, art.cit ('Did LG Starve') and K Jeffery (ed), *The Military Correspondence of Field Marshal Sir Henry Wilson*, 1985, p 22. Also Callwell, *Field Marshal Sir Henry Wilson: His Life and Diaries*, 1927, vol ii, p 98.

77. CAB25/120, LG talking at second meeting, third session of SWC, 31 January 1918, p 3.

78. Full summary of trip in W K Hancock and J van der Poel (eds), *Selections from the Smuts Papers*, 1966, vol iii, 'General Smuts's Mission to Egypt', pp 612–624 (from Smuts papers (Pretoria) vol 20, no. 49).

79. Meinertzhagen diaries, vol 20, 13 February 1918.

80. See Woodward, 'The Imperial Strategist: Jan Christiaan Smuts and British Military Policy 1917–18', *Military History Journal*, December 1981, p 141.

81. Kirke papers, vol vii, p 6.

82. Lloyd George papers, F/2/1/13, Amery to LG, 18 January 1918.

83. CAB24/4/G199, 'Report by General Smuts on his Mission to Egypt', 1 March 1918 (also in WO106/1545).

84. Ibid, pp 2–3.

85. Wilson papers, HHW2/33A/4, Allenby to Wilson, 5 June 1918. (For Pathan discontent see also L/MIL/17/5/3919–3920.)

86. Milner papers, III/B/140, GHQ Egypt to War Office, 1 July 1918 (29% figure here also).

87. Lloyd George, *War Memoirs*, 1938, vol ii, p 1092.

88. Ibid, p 1093.

89. From M Fitzherbert, *The Man Who Was Greenmantle: A Biography of Aubrey Herbert*, 1984, p 241.

Anthony Gross RA CBE: a war artist's diary, Europe 1944–1945

Angela Weight

Angela Weight is Keeper of the Department of Art at the Imperial War Museum

Anthony Gross was born in Dulwich, South London, in 1905, the son of Alexander Gross, a Hungarian-born map publisher of Jewish descent, and Isabelle Crowley, a half Irish Anglo-Italian playwright. The late Phyllis Pearsall was his sister. Educated at Repton School, he studied painting briefly at the Slade and etching at the Central School of Art. Between 1923 and 1926 he moved back and forth between art schools in Paris and Madrid, studying both painting and etching. Throughout the late twenties Gross was mainly resident in France but travelled extensively in Europe and North Africa. In 1930 he met and married Marguerite (Daisy) Florenty, a fashion artist. During the 1930s Gross established his reputation as a painter and etcher, exhibiting his work in London and Paris in both group and one man shows. He knew many of the leading French and expatriate artists in Paris and was intimately involved with the French printmaking scene, a close friend of S W Hayter and an active member of La Jeune Gravure Contemporaine.

In 1932 he completed his first cartoon film, *Une Journée en Afrique*, with Courtland (Hector) Hoppin, a wealthy American photographer. After his second film, *La Joie de Vivre*, was shown to great acclaim in London,Paris and New York in 1935, Gross and Hoppin accepted a contract with Alexander Korda's London Films, but they soon went back to independent production in Paris. Gross was working on an ambitious cartoon-film adaptation of Jules Verne's *A Tour of the World in Eighty Days* when war broke out in 1939; after moving his wife and two children to Daisy's home town of Villeneuve-sur-Lot he returned to London. Here he began work on a new film project, *The Ballad of the Barrage Balloons*, and made watercolours of London preparing for war, while seeking an appointment as a war artist. After completing a contract for the War Artists Advisory Committee but without prospect of further work, Gross went back to France in May 1940; three weeks later Germany invaded. In July Gross and his family escaped to Glasgow on the last boat from Bordeaux.

Once back in London and with his family settled in Flamstead, near St Albans, Gross applied himself to painting with his usual energy; a second exhibition of *London in Wartime* watercolours[1] was held in New York, where his father was now living, and in London at the Leicester Galleries in November and December 1940. The success of this exhibition led to a six-month contract with the WAAC, a contract which was continuously renewed until he resigned as an official war artist in May 1945.

Anthony Gross sailed to Egypt via South Africa in the winter of 1941. Throughout the following year he travelled constantly in Egypt, Palestine, Lebanon, Syria, Persia and Iraq. Although expecting to return to England at this point, he was ordered to India by the War Artists Advisory Committee and sailed from Port Tewfik to Karachi just before Christmas 1942. After six months with the British and Indian Armies in Eastern India and Burma he returned to England via Cairo. During this two year period Gross kept an illustrated diary which described his travels as a war artist.

After his return from India and a much needed rest, Gross was sent to record the preparations and training of the 50th Northumbrian Division and the 1st U S Infantry Division for the invasion of Europe. When D-Day came he sailed with the troops and landed with them after the beach-head had been secured, his sketchbook and materials held over his head. His joy at being back in France glows from a letter he wrote to G C Gregory, Secretary to the War Artists Advisory Committee, on 24 July 1944:

> I am sitting in a wood and it is a very pleasant evening. As you will have heard I had a fairly peaceful landing even though it was distinctly wet. The whole thing was quite astonishing though and fantastic. Quite a feeling of unbelief as I trod the sands of France again and the first evening in a grand Normandy farm with walls built in grey like a castle and of similar dimensions. We knocked back glasses of cider and calvados 'a la Victoire' and rolled over sound asleep after the excitement and the unbelievable exertions of carrying a full pack and painting materials.[2]

Gross's account of his experiences from the Normandy Landings to the final stages of the German war was probably written in note form at the time (since it was at this period that he conceived an ambitious project to publish his war diary as an illustrated édition de luxe) but the existing typescript was made in 1981 while he was following a course of medical treatment at Guy's Hospital and was unable to work.

Anthony Gross, *Jig Beach, looking towards Le Hamel, 7 June 1944.* LD 4461

A War Artist's Diary, Europe 1944-45
by Anthony Gross

D-Day was approaching. I decided to attach myself to the RASC. They had a superb Colonel in charge. After the Battle of Alamein his had been the only unit able to answer Montgomery in the affirmative when he asked them whether they could continue the advance. We were now all down in the New Forest and I remember the day before D-Day being shown a nest which some blue tits had made in a tank, so that tank was left behind and had to catch up later.

We embarked and set sail after a delay. I remember the Needles lit by the evening sun. Next morning we could see the French coast. We disembarked in turns onto landing craft. Our landing craft sailed up and down the coast for two hours. Eventually we were given the signal to come ashore. I held my watercolour paper and colours over my head and jumped overboard into the sea with all the others. The water came up to my armpits. I plodded forward and the water became less deep and eventually I was on dry beach. Some cannon fire on the right hand side about a mile away towards Le Hamel. Then the two intelligence officers who had accompanied me bade me farewell and disappeared as fast as they could. I set myself down on the grass at the top of the beach and made some notes—not easy as I was still soaking wet.

Then I spied a truck driven by a driver I knew from the Army Service Corps. I jumped on it and asked if he would take me to his camp a few hundred yards inland. On arrival at the camp, which was next to a farm, I did a little drawing. The farmer's wife wandered over to look at what I was doing and I asked her if she had any eggs to sell, to which she answered she had and that the Germans were paying her nine francs and she would let me have some at the same price. Then I dug a trench for myself. As I was doing this a rather wild-looking French journalist arrived and asked if he could stay with me. So I handed him my spade and said to him, 'Enlarge this hole for two.' He took the spade and made a couple of digs and then said, 'You know who I am. I am *La France Libre*—on the BBC Foreign programme, *Ici Londres*. I cannot stay here, I must rush off and embrace my countrymen.' Next morning I met a Russian correspondent who was running around with a couple of huge pistols, one in each hand, shooting (so he told me) snipers in church towers.

The next day I went to Bayeux, and helped by my Russian companion found a house with a balcony from where I did a picture of the official liberation of the town of Bayeux. I went on down the road to Tilly and on the outskirts of Bayeux I came to a house where a large number of soldiers, officers and civilians had congregated. I took little notice as I was off to do a drawing but on returning that evening I found a couple of tanks also at the spot.

The CO of the tank said he had come back to make an enquiry because the day before when they were going through Bayeux following the retreating Germans, they had been fired on from the windows of this house. By this time the doors of the house were open and we all went in. There were a dozen or so French girls and men there. We sat down and talked to them. There was a piano and one of the girls played 'Lily Marlene' out of spite. But the tank chaps immediately sang the Desert Rat version of the song with enormous gusto to the discomfiture of the girls, who we had now found out were part of a band of miliciens who were friendly to the Germans. There was a particularly obnoxious man of about sixty amongst them who muttered something about 'Here today, gone tomorrow.' They obviously thought the landing was ephemeral.

My RASC friends now advanced a little more into the bridgehead. They said I could stay with them and lent me a car they had 'recuperated' from the enemy. We were stuck here on the bridgehead for a couple of months. I went into Bayeux and bought a large Port Salut and some Camemberts and posted them at the Army Post Office to Daisy. The postmen were disgusted at the stench of my parcel, but Daisy (together with Winston Churchill) was the first person in England to eat a real French cheese again.

I made myself some *ballances* and went crayfishing. I was stopped after some time by a farmer who said if I went any further along the stream I would come into the German lines. I went home with him and found he worked on a large farm below a chateau and had a large quantity of ducklings nearly ready for the table. I promised to come back and see him.

I asked our Brigadier if he would pose for me. He said he didn't like posing at the start of a campaign, he would prefer the end of it. This rather squashed me. I had to react immediately. So I went and found General Montgomery and asked him the same question. Wouldn't he pose for me surrounded by his counsellors? He said, 'What do you want them for?' I arranged to paint him the next day, but as I was suffering from a tooth I decided to go to a dentist. I found an army dentist in a hamlet and he extracted my tooth, much to the interest of my driver who watched the proceedings through the window.

That night was whisky night again and I had a number of drinks with my companions. Later we were shelled and I transferred to a ditch nearby but during the night I was woken by such a bleeding of my tooth that I could not stop it. I went back to Montgomery and his ADC. As I walked in they went as white as sheets and looked as

Anthony Gross, ***Jerusalem Cross Roads, 13 June 1944.*** **LD 4467**

Anthony Gross, ***151 Brigade Rear Headquarters in the Chateau de Briqueville, Gueron, Normandy, 10 June 1944.*** **LD 4475**

Anthony Gross, *Aunay-sur,-Odon, 13 August 1944.* **LD 4471**

Anthony Gross, *Refugees from Caen and Falaise sheltering in the eleventh century quarries at Fleury-sur-Orne 1944.* **LD 4486**

though they expected me to drop dead. I realised that my face was covered in blood and explained what had happened. I put off my painting appointment, much to the General's displeasure. This was later carried out in a wood nearby when I had recovered.

It was decided that I would go off to Cherbourg and try to buy vegetables for the unit. I set off with a largish truck. The first night I spent in a farm in a Normandy village. We had a splendid meal with the farmer and plenty of cider. As there were some Germans hiding in a forest nearby, I and my driver were put to bed early in cupboards in the wall. We were slightly sozzled and slept well, but I could not help wondering what would have happened if the Germans had come out of the wood and found our truck. It was well hidden behind shrubs anyway. Later we gave up going to Cherbourg as it was still in enemy hands; we bypassed it and bought in the market gardens nearby some lovely cauliflowers, green peas, French beans, artichokes, tomatoes etc, and filled the truck with them. We drove back to camp very pleased with our purchases and started to unload. All the soldiers watched and when the last bag of artichokes was unloaded, they turned and muttered in disgust, 'What, no cabbage?'

The following week we returned, having heard that Cherbourg had capitulated. Here I did a painting and while I was painting my driver came back and told me he had found a beautiful German car belonging to a decamped officer. We went and had a look at it; it was in a long garage beside a cafe. My driver started to back it out. I was terrified that it might be bugged but he said it was impossible. We had got the car about half way out when the door opened and half a dozen Frenchmen came in. When they realised what we were doing, one of them threw himself on his knees spurting tears in all directions and begging me to let him have the car. I was already rather worried about how we were going to get it back to Bayeux and relented, much to my driver's disgust. Then we went to the Citadel and here we saw people loading case upon case of brandy. We parked near an American tank. I waited this side of a canal and my driver went and collected cases of brandy. He handed these to me and I put them in the truck. However we soon realised that as soon as I went back to the canal for the next case the GIs in the tank emptied my truck and put the cases in their tank. So we called a halt and carried the last case of brandy into the truck and drove off.

We then collected some more vegetables and went back to the hotel. Next morning we started for camp. A young Frenchman who knew we were going back to Bayeux asked for a lift. He had been working on a missile site and was anxious to go home. We took him to his father's farm. The family were so happy to see him well and alive that they gave us a great reception. A real banquet. I saw a number of smoked hams hanging in the fireplace and we arranged to return for one of these later. Soon after we arrived at camp and unloaded, I collected all the packets of cigarettes we could lay hands on (about 70) and returned to the farmer and swapped them for the ham.

I went to Caen and painted pictures of the refugees in the Abbaye des Hommes and the caves from which the stones of the Tower of London were quarried. The flies were terrible and the shelling of the town was most disagreeable.

As it was our Colonel's birthday, we decided to go back to Bayeux and buy the ducklings we had seen there, as they would be about ready for eating. A friend whom we nicknamed 'Plate of Bacon', an officer and a delightful man, joined us. When we arrived back at the farm the surroundings were thick with troops and Military Police. We drove into the farm and saw on the verandah of the chateau above a number of Staff Officers. It had become Corps HQ. I rapidly found the farmer and reminded him of the ducks. 'Plate of Bacon' sat in the truck answering the MPs' questions, while I with the farmer twisted the necks of some dozen ducklings much to the amusement of the Staff Officers watching it all from the terrace. We hurried as fast as we could—living off the country was frowned upon by the authorities. Finally, carrying six dead ducks each, the farmer and I clambered into the truck and 'Plate of Bacon' put his foot down on the clutch and we shot out of the hamlet just as a bevy of MPs was bearing down on us. We arrived back at Camp somewhere near Lisieux and had a remarkable birthday party. The Colonel was very touched by our adventure!

As the Americans had by now occupied Brittany I decided to go and paint pictures of the Resistance movement there. I took a truck and went to the headquarters of the Resistance in Rennes. Here I saw a French Resistance colonel and asked his advice and help. Furnished with a number of addresses I first went to Morlaix and met a guide. He took me to Paimpol and then into the interior to meet a resistance group. I did a drawing of the important men and girls of the group.

That night they took me to their headquarters in a farm. Then after we had eaten they said, 'Bring in the prisoner', whereupon a frightened little man was brought in and the leader started questioning him. I said to the leader, 'Please do not do this in front of me. My mission is to draw you, but on no account have I any authority in anything else.' They paused and then said take him away. Afterwards they told me that the accused was a milicien who had executed a number of members of

Anthony Gross, *La Compagnie Tito—members of the maquis in the Maquis de Caillac.* LD 4493

the group. One man had been locked up in a cart for several days with a sow!!

Next morning I left with my guide and travelled through very primitive villages and farms. All the people, men and women, were dressed in Breton clothes. The Germans still held Brest so I came back to Vannes where I again painted a picture of Resistance fighters, in particular a girl messenger covered with bandoliers, grenades and firearms like a Christmas tree.

I heard that the Americans and British were breaking out of the bridgehead—in fact the Americans had reached Strasbourg—so I decided to follow the Armies and make for Paris. I went through Laval and across country until I reached the N20 road at Longjumeau, which I knew well from before the war. Here I was back in the war again. Many soldiers, tanks and vehicles. I enquired whether the road to Paris was open. Then I spied a car with General de Gaulle in it and told my driver to follow it. By this time thousands of people lined the road and as we drove behind de Gaulle we were kissed a hundred times by women and girls and our faces were entirely unrecognisable in lipstick. We arrived at 'La Vache Noir' on the outskirts of Paris and pulled off the road. I spoke to a café owner, whom I had known from before and climbed on to his roof. From here I did a picture of the French Army entering Paris.

When I finished we joined in the liberation and soon found ourselves in the centre of town. We stopped at the Moulin de Belfort and at the counter there were some twenty American GIs and on one side a dozen French Fusiliers Marins with their red pompoms. My driver and I pushed up to the zinc and ordered an aperitif. With the Fusiliers were a number of girls and one Fusilier said to them in a whisper, 'These are the men who count, the British', and a girl answered, 'What a pity he is not Scotch, I would have gone to bed with him for his *jupe*!'

The most extraordinary thing about the sudden liberation of France was the immediate change it brought to the inhabitants. Ruled by the Germans or the Vichy French one day, to wake up the following morning and find the Allies in charge. When I entered Paris on Liberation Day, I saw everywhere girls and men riding bicycles. The girls like in my film *La Joie de Vivre* with their dresses flying around them as they floated past me. When I asked the concierge for a friend of mine, she replied, 'But he is a Jew.' I had known this concierge before the war and she had been so friendly to the family then. But in an instant, almost unnoticeably it changed again, and the street filled full of cars as petrol returned and the concierge realised that being a Jew meant nothing any more. The persons who realised the present was the present were those who had been secretly hoping the Allies would win the war and would return to liberate France. Such was Madame Lefevre of Lefevre-Foinet, a shop for artists' materials, who as I walked into the shop went to a pot and picked out the largest painting brush in it and handed it to me, saying, 'Ca c'est pour vous', and her eyes were shining with joy at the idea that the English and Americans—always her best customers—would at last be back.

I decided to call on an old employee of ours called Régis Anatole in Fontenay. When we found him his joy was immense; we stayed at his house and dined and drank with him and his family. The fame of our arrival spread quickly and two young Alsatian girls in national dress appeared and gave us an inscribed English/French dictionary! The Mayor of Fontenay arrived and we were feted to the sky. At a café where we were being feasted, suddenly there was a deathly silence as the wife of a resistance fighter came in and said they had just brought her husband home dead, killed outside the Chambre des Députés. I rang my brother-in-law Jean Florenty in Montmartre, who said, 'Come along right away, there are no Germans here.' Next day we went to see him and parked our truck outside his shop. As we were talking a man pushed in with a couple of bottles of champagne and said, 'Where are the English?' and handed us one each.

That afternoon we went to the Place de la Concorde for de Gaulle's official entry into the city. We parked in the Square and the truck was immediately covered with spectators—girls, men, old women and children. There must have been a million people around us. Suddenly we heard clapping as a car emerged from the Champs Elysées, carrying General de Gaulle, but this was followed by the noise of firing from the roofs of the Ministère de la Marine on the northern side of the square. I said to my driver, 'Quick, get across the Seine!' The square was covered with sprawling people all afraid of being hit. We threaded our way between them, with the

Anthony Gross, *Caporal Maurice Empereur of the Chasseurs Alpins, on guard in the Little St Bernard's Pass at Seez, Tarantais, France,* 1945. LD 5252

shrieking passengers on the roof crying to be let down, and crossed the river. On the other side we stopped and let our spectators go.

I called on several friends in Paris and then started to look for the TT unit. We found them at Vernon by the bridge over the Seine. They were uncomfortable and worried. We spent a few days with them as I had to do some drawings at the battle scene, where the German army had been smashed by Montgomery. I did this drawing with a sickening feeling in my stomach, the place smelt of death and putrefaction.

Later I headed for Brussels and arrived there the day after the Liberation. I reported to HQ in the town, drew our rations and moved on to the Albert bridge where I caught up with the 50th Northumbrian Division. From here we progressed through Belgium, a very tedious and cold journey. I talked to my Colonel in the RASC and he said he would lend me the little recuperated German car I had used before. He would lend me a driver, who he said was disliked by everybody in the Unit, and with these I set off for Paris. I picked up Jean (Florenty) and then looked for some tyres. We managed to get a full tank for the car and a few extra jerry cans, which we swopped for tyres at a garage [whose] owner I knew from before the war, and set off for Lyons. Soon we were low on petrol. We were following a route we thought was still being used by the Americans but it was abandoned now. We arrived at a large field, in the middle of which was one black American soldier guarding two jerry cans of petrol. My driver said, 'Leave this to me. I'm good with the blackies.' He wandered over to the guard and after a short while they returned, the guard and my driver carrying a jerry can each!

With this we made good going till we reached [blank]. We were low again and I called on a French unit who told me they were very low on petrol as well. We obtained another two jerry cans from them, crossed the mountain and reached the main road up from the Mediterranean to Germany. My driver was talking to a GI and when we drove up he saluted me and filled the car up. When we had driven on I asked my driver what he had told the GI: 'That you was in Security and Jean Florenty was a French Secret Service Agent!'

We drove down to Avignon and crossed the Rhone. The road was covered with smashed or abandoned German equipment. At Agen we were stopped by a gang of Freedom Fighters, who asked for our papers, of which we had none, so we handed them packets of American cigarettes. This delighted them, and then one said, 'Surely it is you, Jean Florenty?' and we went with half the gang hanging on the outside of the car to Villeneuve. Here we met Daisy's father and niece and stayed a few days.

The only fuel we could obtain here was turpentine and we drove on this to Causade. Here we lost another tyre. We called in at the Town Hall and found a guard on the doors. We explained our plight, but at that moment an officer appeared and said to us, 'Soyez les bienvenus.' Le General, for whom they were waiting, had just rung through to say he could not come, and what better guests could they possibly have than the British. So we were feasted royally and at four that afternon when we left, there in front of the Town Hall was our little car, guarded by soldiers, waiting for us with four brand new tyres and a full tank. We said goodbye and set off for Paris.

In Paris, while we were walking down the Champs Elysees, we were suddenly passed by a full (British) colonel. A moment later an officer came up and said, 'You will report to my office in an hour's time. You will be on a charge, scruffily dressed in Paris, when we, the English, are in full view!' We left for Belgium immediately.

We were in Holland during a rather dreary winter. Then I returned home.

I went back again to France to do a series of pictures on the French frontier from Nice to Hanover: a picture of an American soldier guarding a bridge at Wurtzberg. The bar and the interior of a cellar and an American soldier lying in a mess of straw and empty bottles saying, 'I cannot understand how people can drink this sour stuff', and passing out. Heidelberg pictures—crossing the Rhine. The German girls looking after our barracks so thoroughly. Then Luneberg and the end!

Acknowledgement

The typescript of Anthony Gross's diary has been edited for publication by Angela Weight with the permission of Mr Peter Gross and Mrs Mary West, the son and daughter of the artist.

Notes

1. The first was at the Leicester Galleries in February 1940.
2. Anthony Gross to G C Gregory, Secretary to the War Artists Advisory Committee, 24 July 1944.

'. . . it looked more natural': Miss Rosie Newman's colour film of the Second World War

Jane Fish

Rosie Newman with her Kodak Model K 16mm camera, c. 1940. HU 65920

When considering film of Britain during the Second World War the images that usually spring to mind are black and white, as the vast majority of the film record of life on the home front was shot on black and white stock. However, there was a small amount of film, mostly amateur, shot on colour stock. One such film is the remarkable colour record of the British home front by amateur filmmaker Miss Rosie Newman. Talking to her interviewer in 1980 Rosie Newman remarked, 'I never realised the unique value of shooting in colour, I just thought it looked more natural'.[1] These modest words belie the significance of her colour film and her considerable achievement in producing her personal film, *Britain at War.*[2]

Miss Rosie Violet Nina Millicent Newman (1896-1988) was one of five children of the wealthy Bavarian born banker Sir Sigismund Neumann[3] and Anna Allegra Hakim from Alexandria. She was presented at court, known in London society and well travelled. In 1928, when planning a motor trip through Morocco, she decided to take up what was then considered the latest amusing hobby, amateur cinematography. For this trip she purchased her first 16mm camera from the leading London supplier, Wallace Heaton of New Bond Street. It was from films shot in Morocco that she produced her first edited film, a short black and white record of her holiday,[4] an amateur travelogue which was typical of wealthy travellers of the period.[5]

Rosie Newman gained confidence with the new medium and on her more extensive trip to India in 1935

Jane Fish is Production Information Officer, Film and Video Archive, at the Imperial War Museum.

she took her camera and a supply of Kodacolor[6] film, a 16mm colour film stock. As a guest of the Viceroy, Lord Willingdon, Rosie Newman travelled extensively, visiting Bombay, New Delhi, Calcutta, Benares (Varanasi), Darjeeling and Peshawar on the Afghanistan border. Although touring in wealthy circles, her filming in India was not limited to the grandeur and beauty of British Residencies and Maharajahs' palaces, but, as with her later productions, she was also interested in the country and its people. 'I wasn't particularly interested in cocktail parties and things. I wanted to see the people and their customs, and how they lived . . . yes, but of course the contacts I did make at the cocktail parties helped me to get around the country.'[7] (This talent for making useful contacts was to prove invaluable in her wartime filming.)

According to an article published in *The Lady*[8] in 1948, Lord Willingdon, impressed by the brilliance of the colour stock and the quality of Rosie Newman's camera work, suggested that she should show her films to a wider audience. From her Indian films Rosie Newman produced *Glimpses of India* and *Further Glimpses of India*,[9] and began to screen these films in a variety of locations, the homes of friends, hotels and public halls, with the proceeds from the sale of tickets going to charity (for example, King Emperor's Indian Anti-Tuberculosis Fund and the British Red Cross). Throughout the mid-1930s she continued to travel with her 16mm camera and produced further colour films, *Across the Border* (Scotland 1936) and *To The Land of the Pharaohs* (c 1937)[10] which she also exhibited publicly. In February 1936, as a result of her growing reputation as an amateur filmmaker, Rosie Newman was elected fellow of the Royal Geographic Society.

At the outbreak of the Second World War, Rosie Newman joined the Women's Voluntary Service (WVS) and continued to show her films for charity and as entertainment for the troops at home. However, she felt she could do more for the war effort and in early 1940 it was suggested to her that she might take her films to France to entertain troops of the British Expeditionary Force (BEF) and to raise funds for French war charities. With admirable persistence and the invaluable help and advice of influential friends—'numerous letters of introduction were given to me by many kind friends whose unfailing interest was a source of great encouragement'—[11] Rosie Newman organised her trip to France under the auspices of the War Office, the French Red Cross and the YMCA and obtained all the necessary permits and visas. Her chauffeur-cum-projectionist Bob Fennymore, entrusted with the suitcases and twelve large wooden packing cases of film equipment, set off for France by sea on 28 March 1940. Rosie Newman followed two days later, flying from Heston to Le Bourget on 30 March, accompanied by her friend Lady Joan Birkbeck.

Rosie Newman, Bob Fennymore and the equipment prior to leaving for France, March 1940. HU 66416

Once in France, Rosie Newman and her party travelled from Paris to the French Riviera for a screening of her films at the Casino in Cannes on 11 April to raise funds for the French Red Cross. Whilst in the South of France she filmed, on 16mm Kodachrome[12] colour stock, various scenes with a contingent of French Senegalese troops and French troops on leave. In mid-April, Lady Joan returned to England, and Rosie Newman travelled back to Paris in order to arrange her film shows for the BEF. During her stay in the French capital she undertook several more charity film shows and also found time to enjoy Parisian society and visit the races at Longchamps. However, by early May, Rosie Newman began to be more aware of the worsening military situation. 'I had been warned by people who were really "in the know", that the "blitzkrieg" was likely to break out at any moment, it was already May and they had advised me not to delay my departure for England much longer, but being determined to give the film shows to the BEF . . .'.[13] Rosie Newman spent two days with the BEF showing her films to packed and enthusiastic audiences and filming some brief scenes of the troops in training. She returned to Paris just after the German invasion of Holland and was now certain it was time for her to leave France. Rosie Newman arranged to depart by air a couple of days later, probably on 13 May, 'Fearing to be delayed by a warning I left for the aerodrome in plenty of time'[14] and according to her own account 'it was actually the last civilian machine to leave'.[15] Bob Fennymore and the equipment left Paris the day before to cross the Channel by boat and eventually arrived back in England some four days later. Miraculously the films shot in France also reached England weeks later. 'By then I had given up hope of ever seeing the films again which I had taken in France, when a parcel, consisting of two old biscuit tins, the only things I could find to pack the films in, was among one of the last to arrive at the French Embassy. I was delighted as the films had been taken under the greatest difficulties.'[16] (Later Rosie Newman combined her 1940 film of wartime France with pre-war footage, producing a film entitled *The France I Knew*.)[17]

In mid-June 1940, a short while after her return from France, Rosie Newman decided upon the most ambitious project of her amateur filmmaking career, a record of wartime England. 'Invasion seemed imminent. Britain found herself alone in the world struggle. . . . It was at this crisis that I really decided to make a film of England at war. Perhaps if I had realised the difficulties I should encounter I might have hesitated before coming to this decision; but once it was made, events seemed to push me towards my new enterprise. Although it was some time later before I actually commenced doing the film in earnest'.[18]

In 1941 she began filming, ignoring advice previously given in *Amateur Cine World [The Only Journal Solely Devoted to Substandard Cinematography]*,[19] a popular monthly magazine providing a wealth of detailed advice on every aspect of amateur film making and presentation. 'Let not your cine camera be seen anywhere near the following; . . . aerodrome or seaplane station; assembly of forces . . . factory . . . dockyard, harbour . . .; vessel of war or any vessel or vehicle engaged in the transport of supplies or personnel; aircraft . . .'[20] Instead, Rosie Newman used all her contacts and tenacity to obtain the necessary official permissions to film in many of the areas *Amateur Cine World* proscribed.

Her old friend and stalwart supporter of her filmmaking, Lord Willingdon, wrote to the Ministry of Information (MoI) to enlist their help and support. In reply he received the following from Sir Walter Monckton, Deputy Director-General of the MoI,[21] dated 28 March 1941: 'Thank you for your note about Miss Newman. I found that she has already been in touch with the Films Division here who think highly of her work and would like to give her every possible help . . . I am giving instructions that she is to be backed up as far as possible.'

With the support of the MoI, the assistance of influential friends and following one of her favourite maxims, 'never take no for an answer', Rosie Newman obtained a Photography Permit to film in London and the necessary permissions to film from the Air Ministry, the Ministry of Aircraft Production, Headquarters Eastern Command, Canadian Military Headquarters (London) and the Admiralty. Apparently the only permission refused to her was from the Fleet Air Arm regarding her request to film on board an aircraft carrier.

The permissions she received required her to submit her undeveloped films for processing and censorship and often included a written list of restrictions and 'Do's and Don'ts'. For example, the permit issued by the Directorate of Public Relations, Air Ministry included obvious security measures such as not identifying locations, units, armaments and the names of personnel, plus advice on conforming to the discipline and etiquette of the station and making filming requests reasonable and clear.[22]

After her earlier success with colour filming Rosie Newman chose to shoot her film of wartime England on 16mm Kodachrome, the Kodak colour stock that had replaced the earlier Kodacolor. However, this choice presented her with one of her greatest problems, as, although marketed in Britain from 1936, 16mm Kodachrome stock was produced in America and had already become very difficult to obtain in wartime Britain.

Canadian troops on exercises. Soldiers wearing full protective clothing laying a paper carpet over 'gas contaminated ground', near Bordon, Hampshire, 1/2 July 1941. FLM 2872

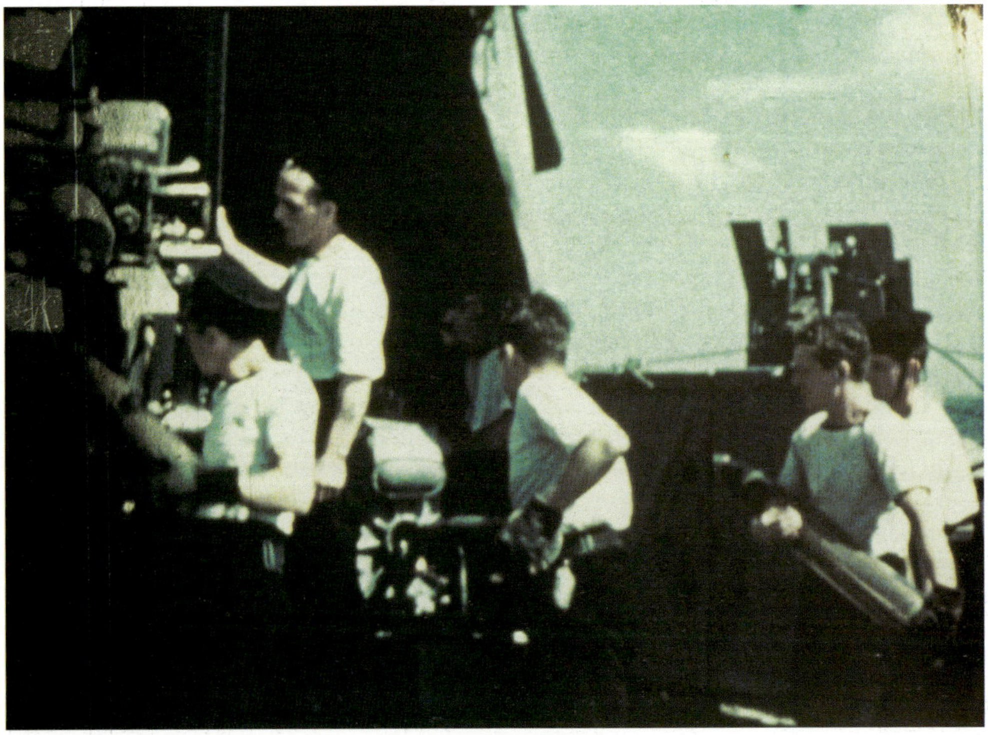

Sailors manning the twin 4-inch guns, HMS *Berkeley* (L.17) out of Portsmouth, 27 June 1941. FLM 2874

RAF personnel queuing at a NAAFI wagon, RAF Digby, 21 or 22 July 1941. FLM 2873

Sailors playing 'uckers' (ludo) on board HMS *Berkeley* (L. 17) out of Portsmouth, 27 June 1941. FLM 2877

Her contacts at the Films Division of the MoI did what they could to help, with R Nunn May supplying her with a letter of introduction and support dated 28 June 1941. 'Miss R Newman is engaged upon the production of a film on 16mm which is to be shown in aid of the Red Cross and it will be appreciated if, for the purposes of this production, she may be supplied with 16mm Kodachrome film.' Mr Nunn May judiciously added in his covering letter of the same date, 'The position with regard to film stock is, however, becoming increasingly difficult, and even this note will not conjure into existence film stock which is not in this country.'[23] Again Rosie Newman called upon her friends for help. 'Kodachrome films were unobtainable in England, even with a permit from the Ministry of Information. An officer compared it to running out of ammunition! However, I managed to collect some films from friends, but not as many as I could wish; so I had to severely ration myself.'[24] However, she was also in the extremely advantageous position of being able to obtain some colour film stock directly from North America. 'I had very good friends within the American and Canadian Military Attaches who saw to it that the odd roll came across the Atlantic.'[25]

The earliest scenes for her new production were of members of 'J' Zone Home Guard, London District, on 5 January 1941, in training and on the march. However, the scenes of the Home Guard are not typical of her filming. As with her previous productions, Rosie Newman's interest was more personal, recording not only a country mobilised for war, but people and the routines of daily life. The material she filmed at RAF Digby on 21–22 August 1941 features not only the Spitfires and personnel of 412 Squadron, Royal Canadian Air Force, but also scenes of daily life on the station with shots of the servicing of aircraft and 'tea time' at the NAAFI wagon.

Rosie Newman filmed in Portsmouth in June 1941 recording scenes of members of the Womens Royal Naval Service at their quarters in St Michael's Road. Remarkably, she was also allowed to film on board the Hunt class escort destroyer HMS *Berkeley* (L. 17) at sea out of Portsmouth, on 27 June 1941, an extremely unusual event for any amateur filmmaker, let alone a woman. The original permission received from the Admiralty was to film in Portsmouth docks. In an interview for the *John Dunn Show* on BBC Radio 2, on 12 January 1977, Rosie Newman explained how she came to be on board the destroyer. Apparently she had met an Admiral Brook[26] at a luncheon party and after chatting with him and discussing her film and her plans for her visit to Portsmouth he arranged the trip on board HMS *Berkeley*. This extraordinary event of a civilian camerawoman on board a Royal Navy ship did not go unnoticed by the dock authorities at the time. '. . . after being out in a destroyer a naval policeman came on board and said "No woman is allowed on board, especially with a camera". I left it to the Captain to settle.'[27] Rosie Newman spent the day on board HMS *Berkeley* and the Captain and crew gave her every co-operation (with the Captain, Lieutenant Commander H G Walters, even going so far as to lend her a pair of his trousers, which were more suitable for moving around the ship). Her extensive footage, shot at sea, included the firing of the twin 4-inch guns, the launch of the ship's whaler, making smoke, distribution of the rum ration and the presentation of medals to members of the crew. Rosie Newman also filmed informal shots of the crew eating, and playing with the ship's puppy, a game of 'uckers' (Ludo) and the distribution of sea boot socks.

Rosie Newman also filmed with the Army, accompanying Lieutenant-General McNaughton, Commander of the Canadian Forces Overseas, and a contingent of Canadian troops on exercises near Bordon, Hampshire, on 1 and 2 July 1941. Whilst with the Canadians her camera did not remain with the General and his officers but concentrated on the ordinary soldiers, filming Valentine tanks, infantry, field telephones and some unusual footage of a gas contamination drill in the field including scenes of soldiers in full protective clothing laying a paper carpet over 'contaminated' ground.

With her Photography Permit Rosie Newman filmed the London Blitz in the spring of 1941, producing some particularly striking and evocative night shots of burning blitzed buildings. She also worked extensively during the day, filming the damage to houses, a furniture depository, St Thomas's Hospital and to many religious buildings including St James's Piccadilly, Southwark Roman Catholic Cathedral and minor damage to St Paul's Cathedral. The surprising sight of a woman with a film camera was often a cause of curiosity. 'Of course I must have looked an unusual sight filming the Blitz and its aftermath . . . but in the main when people realised what I was doing they gave me every consideration.'[28] A policeman after checking her permit remarked 'I didn't know girls were employed on jobs like this.'[29] The London scenes include not only damage to the city but also everyday life, queues, rubble, men at work, piles of salvage in Hyde Park, an ARP hut, a stretcher party and also a subject of obvious particular personal appeal, wartime shop windows. Many of the scenes were filmed in and around Piccadilly and Bond Street, an area with which Rosie Newman was most familiar, (until she was 'bombed-out' she had a home at 146 Piccadilly and later became a resident of the Dorchester Hotel, Park Lane).

Policeman examining Rosie Newman's Photography Permit, London 1941. FLM 2870

Other 1941 sequences include film of stately homes familiar to Rosie Newman from pre-war days: the private house of Foxwarren Park, with staged shots of gas masks and an air raid shelter, and Hever Castle, home to many evacuees, with informal scenes of soldiers and sailors visiting their evacuated families. Later she filmed at Rushbrooke Auxiliary Hospital, a Jacobean Hall near Bury St Edmunds, with shots of patients in the oak panelled wards, playing cards, eating and taking part in group remedial exercise sessions in the grounds.

With the support and co-operation of the Ministry of Aircraft Production Rosie Newman shot a substantial amount of footage, both black and white and colour, of work at the Phillips and Powis aircraft factory at Reading on 27 August 1941. Her footage includes scenes of manufacture, aircraft components and completed aircraft including Miles Masters resplendent in their training yellow underpaint. She also filmed workers enjoying a cup of tea and the elephantine image of a barrage balloon protecting the factory.

In September 1941, whilst in Scotland, Rosie Newman travelled to Haddington to film lumberjacks from British Honduras. The men proved most willing subjects for her camera and she filmed them at work in the forest producing pit props, posing with their gas masks and in their tented camp with brief shots of an exhibition boxing match staged for her benefit.

The first version of her film entitled *England at War* was completed in 1942 and screened to an audience from the top echelons of wartime London society at a private view at the Dorchester Hotel on 7 May 1942. Her guests included the Lord Mayor and Lady Mayoress of London, the Brazilian Ambassador, the Marchioness of Willingdon and Archduke Robert of Austria. This social event was reviewed in *The Tatler:* 'An interesting occasion was the showing of Miss Rosie Newman's film *England at War* at the Dorchester. She made the film, which is all in colour, herself; it covers the whole war effort and includes some excellent blitz pictures about which the audience was especially congratulatory, and some lovely shots taken from a destroyer, Miss Newman being the only woman actually allowed to patrol in one.'[30] A subsequent public showing at the Dorchester Hotel on 3 June 1942 raised the then substantial amount of £362 for the British Red Cross.

The film was presented in what had by now become her traditional format, beginning with a brief spoken introduction by Rosie Newman followed by the projection of *England at War* by her chauffeur, Bob Fennymore. The silent film was accompanied by a selection of classical, British folk and patriotic music played on a dual turn-table gramophone operated by Rosie Newman herself. For this film she experimented with a new form of accompaniment, including a recording of part of a poem, 'Big Steamers' by Elsie Bambridge, over a section of the HMS *Berkeley* sequence. As with her previous productions, Rosie Newman wrote a short book about her filming under the same title[31] which was sold at her screenings by willing helpers.

England at War was produced entirely by Rosie Newman. The film consisted, predominantly, of footage shot by her, supplemented by a very small amount of black and white official footage supplied by the MoI. Rosie Newman edited the film herself and also created the colour captions which introduced each sequence (for obvious security reasons these captions did not identify locations, dates, units etc).

Later in 1942 she changed the title of her film to *Britain at War* (although, always aware of the proprieties, she changed the title back to *England at War* for a screening to the Royal Society of St George on 5 May 1943), and during the latter part of 1942 and throughout 1943 she continued to screen the film to a variety of audiences both civilian and military.

In 1943 she returned to her films shot in France in 1940, combining them with film of the Free French Navy shot in Plymouth in December 1940 and earlier Kodacolor footage of pre-war holidays in Le Touquet, Paris and on the French Riviera to produce *The France I Knew.* This film

Servicemen with their evacuated families, Hever Castle, Kent, 1941. FLM 2871

Patients with leg wounds undertaking remedial exercises in the grounds of Rushbrooke Auxiliary Hospital, Bury St Edmunds, Suffolk, May 1942. FLM 2886

received its first public screening at the Dorchester Hotel on 15 February 1944, raising funds for the Association des Amis des Volontaires Francais. The well attended social event was also reviewed in *The Tatler.* 'There was a terribly nostalgic feeling in the hearts of everyone who attended the colour film *The France I Knew* . . . It was quite painful to have one's memories revived of Le Touquet, Cannes and Paris as they used to be. The second part of this admirable colour-film showed France during 1940, showing as it does France and her soldiers in war days.'[32]

In autumn 1944, after the D-Day Landings, Rosie Newman resolved to add further scenes to *Britain at War.* 'I felt I must finish the job to which so long before I had put my hand.'[33] She obtained a permit to film at Southampton Docks on 13 December 1944 and recorded scenes of troops embarking for Europe and landing-craft in the port. She also received permission from the Air Ministry to film the disembarkation of wounded at RAF Down Ampney between 17 and 19 December 1944.

Rosie Newman filmed the concluding scenes for her final version of *Britain at War* in London in June 1946, producing vivid colour footage of a city bedecked by flags and long shots of the Victory Parade. On adding these final scenes she re-titled her film *Britain Through The War,* although later she reverted to *Britain at War* and in 1948 produced a second edition of the book of her film, now also entitled *Britain at War.*[34] With this film Rosie Newman had managed to achieve what, in early 1940, *Amateur Cine World* had considered 'the almost impossible'. 'Straightforward documentary presentation will prove almost impossible owing to the fact that it is forbidden to photograph anything directly connected with war and defence work, troop movements or actions. Thus, documentary films of war life will have to be patched together from such scenes as are allowed to be taken, and they will mainly consist of harmless street scenes and the close-ups of various war-time gadgets and requisites such as gas masks, rations cards etc. etc.'[35]

Rosie Newman was a self-taught amateur camerawoman who practised her pastime with skill and dedication. Her experience and reputation as a pre-war amateur filmmaker, combined with her privileged position in society, her redoubtable persistence and unquestionably an amount of personal charm enabled her to produce a unique record of parts of the British home front during the Second World War. For Rosie Newman her wartime filmmaking was not only an interesting hobby and one which raised considerable funds for charity, but also her singular contribution to the war effort.

Britain at War is by no means the only amateur colour film shot in Britain during the Second World War

Rosie Newman introducing a screening of *Britain at War,* 5 March 1945. HU 66433

Mrs Churchill will be present at the film we hope you will be able to come.

Y.W.C.A.

Y.W.C.A. WARTIME FUND

(Registered under the War Charities Act, 1940)

President: MRS. CHURCHILL

"BRITAIN AT WAR"

An absorbing, inspiring, All-Colour Film to which has been added new and exceptional scenes from D-Day, 1944, Taken by MISS ROSIE NEWMAN, F.R.G.S.

to be shewn in

The Assembly Hall, Royal Empire Society

Northumberland Avenue, W.C. 2

on

MONDAY, March 5th, from 5.45 to 7.30 p.m.

The entire proceeds of the performance for the Fund

INTRODUCTION BY THE RT. HON. THE EARL OF CLARENDON, K.G., G.C.V.O.

PATRONS

THE DUCHESS OF ATHOLL, D.B.E., D.C.L.
MRS. DREXEL BIDDLE
MAUD, COUNTESS OF FITZWILLIAM
THE HON. LADY FORSTER, G.B.E.
LADY HAMOND-GRAEME
THE MARCHIONESS OF LINLITHGOW, C.I.
THE COUNTESS OF MIDLETON
LADY SINCLAIR
LADY SYKES
THE MAYOR AND MAYORESS OF THE CITY OF WESTMINSTER
MARIE, MARCHIONESS OF WILLINGDON, C.I., G.B.E.

COMMITTEE

Chairman: LADY ALLARDYCE, C.B.E.

MRS. BENN
MRS. MERVYN COX
LADY DALRYMPLE-CHAMPNEYS
MRS. WARREN PEARL
LADY PRICE
LADY ROOTES
MRS. WASHINGTON SINGER
LADY WARD

TICKETS

Gallery: £1 1s. Stalls: £3 3s.; 12/6;
5/- (unreserved)

can be obtained from

LADY ALLARDYCE, Y.W.C.A. National Headquarters, Great Russell Street, W.C.1 (Museum 3111)
MISS ROSIE NEWMAN, The Dorchester Hotel, London, W. I. (Mayfair 8888)

Morrish & Co., 56 Great Titchfield Street, W.1

An advertisement for a screening of *Britain at War,* annotated by Rosie Newman.

and Rosie Newman was not the only amateur camerawoman filming in Britain at that time. (The Imperial War Museum holds many other fine examples of Second World War amateur cinematography including colour films shot by Kathleen Lockwood in Holmfirth and Arthur Green in London.) The particular significance of Rosie Newman's *Britain at War* lies in the combination of its quality, content and colour.

The quality of *Britain at War* is extremely good throughout. The images are clear, well composed and well shot, with the skilled editing and captioning producing a fluid narrative to the documentary. Rosie Newman's experience as a pre-war filmmaker and exhibitor gave her a practised eye and an understanding of the techniques of amateur cinematography which she fully utilised when producing her wartime film.

The breadth of *Britain at War* transcends a recording of personal experience and the familiar, often the mainstay of the amateur filmmaker. Obviously, some of the subjects were chosen for their familiarity and ease of access: London's West End, stately homes and the lumberjacks from British Honduras at work in an area of Scotland familiar to Rosie Newman's family, but the scope of her production was far more ambitious. Rosie Newman strove to record every aspect of wartime Britain which was of interest to her and which could be made accessible, limited only by the necessary official permissions. Despite her social background *Britain at War* is not concerned with Generals and 'the great and the good' but more interested in the routines of everyday life for both her military and civilian subjects. Most of her shots are simple and personal, allowing the viewer to relate to the images; the saving of a single chair from a bomb damaged building, women and children talking in a queue, workmen drinking tea, a lone airman sitting writing a letter and sailors playing a board game. Rosie Newman filmed with an uncomplicated eye, recording both the ordinary and extraordinary.

Her previous experience of using colour film stock gave her the confidence and the ambition to continue to film in colour. Despite the problems of obtaining Kodachrome stock she persevered, resorting to black and white film for only a few sequences, mostly interior shots with low light levels. The uncommon colour footage gives an intimacy and immediacy of image, in comparison with the more common and familiar black and white images of the period which often distance the viewer from the subject. The colours of uniforms, equipment, aircraft, civilian clothes, shop windows and flags often

Lumberjacks from British Honduras piling timber, Haddington, Scotland, September 1941. FLM 2936

Newspaper seller, London 1941. FLM 2883

Bomb site off Piccadilly, with passing bus, London 1941. FLM 2884

Night shot of burning bomb damaged building, London 1941. FLM 2869

surprise, reminding the viewer that, while wartime Britain was usually filmed in black and white, the country mobilised, trained, fought and endured in colour.

Despite her modesty regarding the value of her colour record Rosie Newman could not have been unaware of the high regard in which her film work was held. During the 1940s she was lauded by the London society press and her peers, with such notables as Clementine Churchill and HM Queen Mary attending her film screenings. Her peculiar contribution to the war effort was recognised with her invitation to a luncheon at the Mansion House to meet HRH the Princess Royal at a social occasion 'to bring together women leaders of the war effort of the British Empire and Allies' on 16 February 1943.

Over thirty years after the end of the Second World War, Rosie Newman was again recognised for her achievement as a wartime filmmaker. Her films were not located by Thames Television in their trawl for footage for their acclaimed documentary series *The World at War* (1974), but after she deposited her material with the Imperial War Museum in 1975, extracts from *Britain at War* were included in the 1977 BBC Television series *Secret War.* Her colour London Blitz scenes promoted considerable press interest. 'There were at least three women in this war who were themselves secret weapons . . . Miss Rosie Newman was shooting the blitz in colour which was, in theory, impossible. A well-off well-connected lady is hard for authority to handle. You don't know what to do with her, or if you do you don't' . . .[36] Later, as a result of this publicity, Rosie Newman became the subject of a short Anglia Television documentary.[37]

For many years after the end of the war Rosie Newman continued to show her pre-war and wartime films for charity, raising funds for numerous organisations including the Red Cross, The Distressed Gentlefolk's Aid Association and the Invalid Children's Aid Association. She continued to travel with her camera and produced several more short colour films, two of which are also part of the collection of her material held at the Imperial War Museum.[38] However, *Britain at War* was undoubtedly her 'finest hour' as an amateur filmmaker and, as stated in *The Times* more than fifty years ago, 'The film must rank as one of the most interesting and comprehensive amateur documentaries produced during the war'.[39]

Acknowledgements

With thanks to Orlagh Mulcahy and David Kenton. With special thanks to Mrs Caroline Crawshaw and Sir Francis Newman for the loan of albums and documents owned by the late Miss Rosie Newman.

Notes

1. Miss Rosie Newman's interview with David Kenton, Anglia Television, 14 February 1980, for *A Bygone Special: Miss Rosie Newman—A Colour Supplement,* IWM Sound Archive ref 13843/3.
2. *Britain at War* (post–1946 version), IWM Film and Video Archive ref MGH 3773.
3. Sir Sigismund Neumann was created baronet in 1912; the family name later anglicised to Newman.
4. The first part of *Morocco 1928 + 1966,* IWM Film and Video Archive ref MGH 3768.
5. Patricia R Zimmerman, *Reel Families: A Social History of Amateur Film,* Indiana University Press, USA, 1995. Chapter 3 'Professional Results with Amateur Ease'.
6. Kodacolor—a three-colour additive lenticular process, first introduced in 1928. (For further technical information see *The Focal Encyclopedia of Film and Television Techniques,* Focal Press, London and New York, 1969, pp 172–173.) Today Kodacolor presents considerable technical problems with regard to its preservation and duplication on to other media.
7. Newman interview.
8. Elizabeth Coxhead, 'Historian in Celluloid', *The Lady,* 17 June 1948.
9. *Glimpses of India,* IWM Film and Video Archive ref MGH 3769. *Further Glimpses of India,* IWM Film and Video Archive ref MGH 3770.
10. *Across the Border* (travels in Scotland), IWM Film and Video Archive ref MGH 3776. *To the Land of the Pharaohs,* IWM Film and Video Archive ref MGH 3771.
11. Rosie Newman, *The France I Knew,* Chiswick Press, London, 1944, p 8.
12. Kodachrome—a tripack colour process, first introduced in 1935.
13. Rosie Newman, *The France I Knew,* p 36.
14. Ibid, p 41.
15. Ibid, p 41.
16. Ibid, p 42.
17. *The France I Knew,* IWM Film and Video Archive ref MGH 3772.
18. Rosie Newman, *Britain at War,* Max Love, London (?), 1948, p 6.
19. Substandard or narrow-gauge—terms used to describe all film widths smaller than the professional 35mm standard width.
20. Gordon S Malthouse (The Editor), 'What Shall I Film in War-time?', *Amateur Cine World,* December 1939.
21. Letter from Walter Monckton, 28 March 1941—held in Rosie Newman's *England our England* Album, property of the Newman family.
22. Directorate of Public Relations, Air Ministry pass no 5340, 19 August 1941—held in Rosie Newman's *England our England* Album.
23. Letters from R Nunn May—held in Rosie Newman's *England our England* Album.
24. Rosie Newman, *Britain at War,* p 28.
25. Newman interview.
26. Probably Rear-Admiral Sir Basil Vernon Brooke Retd, of the Royal Household.
27. Newman interview.
28. Newman interview.
29. Rosie Newman, *Britain at War,* p 21.
30. *The Tatler and Bystander,* Vol CLXIV, No 2134, 20 May 1942.
31. Rosie Newman, *Britain at War,* Max Love, London (?), 1948.
32. *The Tatler and Bystander,* Vol CLXXI, No 2227, 1 March 1944.
33. Rosie Newman, *Britain at War,* p 50.
34. Ibid.
35. Alex Strasser, 'War-time plots for filming', *Amateur Cine World,* January 1940.
36. Nancy Banks-Smith ,'The Secret War of Dr Jones', *The Guardian,* 6 January 1977.
37. *A Bygones Special: Miss Rosie Newman—A Colour Supplement,* Anglia Television, 1980, IWM Film and Video Archive ref MGH 1928.
38. *A Flying Visit to Yugoslavia* (1956), IWM Film and Video Archive ref MGH 3774. *By Air to Cyprus and Athens* (c. 1953), IWM Film and Video Archive ref MGH 3774.
39. 'Britain at War', (not attributed), *The Times,* 6 March 1945.

Selfridges department store, decked with Allied flags, Oxford Street, London, 8 June 1946. FLM 2876

'KITCHENER WANTS YOU' and 'Daddy, what did YOU do in the Great War?': the myth of British recruiting posters.

Nicholas Hiley

Dr Nicholas Hiley is Head of Information at the British Universities Film and Video Council.

The vivid recruiting posters of the Parliamentary Recruiting Committee, or PRC, have provided us with some of the most powerful images of British society during the First World War. The PRC's poster campaign has not only come to be regarded as vital to the mobilisation of popular support for the war, but two of the designs attributed to it, Alfred Leete's 'KITCHENER WANTS YOU' and Savile Lumley's 'Daddy, what did YOU do in the Great War?', have risen to become icons of twentieth-century British history. Representing on the one hand the direct order to enlist, and on the other a more subtle form of indirect pressure exerted through the family, they seem to demonstrate both the government's unscrupulous manipulation of public opinion, and the essential impotence of the individual when faced with the power of the modern state.[1]

The enormous scale of the PRC's poster campaign was certainly impressive, for according to its records the main recruiting drive involved the production of more than 140 different poster designs, from which no fewer than 5.7 million full-size posters were printed, along with 550,000 smaller strip posters 'for use on taxi-cabs and trams and in railway carriages', and 450,000 show cards 'for hanging up in public institutions, offices, shops and houses'. This enormous output reflected the personal nature of the campaign, for most of the PRC designs were issued in single-sheet Double Crown size (30ins × 20 ins), rather than in the larger 8-sheet (80 ins × 60 ins), 16-sheet (120 ins × 80 ins) or 32-sheet (120 ins × 160 ins) sizes favoured by commercial advertisers. PRC posters did appear in large numbers on the hoardings, but they were also to be seen in factories and shops, and considerable help was acknowledged 'from railway and tramway companies, labour exchanges, banks, hotels, public libraries, co-operative societies, and various other institutions.'[2]

A recruiting campaign which ran for little more than a year, and yet involved an average of three new designs a week and a total production of 6.7 million posters and show cards, was undoubtedly an enormous achievement and certainly dwarfed all previous publicity campaigns run by the British government. However, the sheer volume of the PRC's output has served to distort the picture of wartime recruiting, for it has helped to conceal the complexity of the underlying debate, and has forced single images such as Leete's 'KITCHENER WANTS YOU' and Lumley's 'Daddy, what did YOU do in the Great War?' far out of their historical context. Most descriptions of the

Alfred Leete's *KITCHENER WANTS YOU* from 1914, a poster that has become one of the iconic images of the Great War. Department of Art, 2734

Savile Lumley's *Daddy, what did YOU do in the Great War?*, which the Parliamentary Recruiting Committee issued in March 1915 as poster PRC 79. Department of Art, 0311

campaign stress the importance of these two designs, but the truth is that the closer we look at the contemporary evidence, the less impressive do they actually become, and the further removed do their slogans and their sentiments seem from the common experience of wartime enlistment.

The PRC's poster campaign was originally designed not to create enthusiasm for the war, but to sustain it. In August 1914 the Secretary of State for War, Lord Kitchener, asked for 100,000 new recruits to form the basis of his new armies, and within weeks almost 300,000 men had come forward in an unprecedented show of patriotism. By the beginning of September 1914 the Prime Minister was having to admit that 'recruiting is going on so fast and furiously . . . that it is becoming a question whether we should not rather try for the moment to damp it down,' and the War Office was forced to raise its minimum physical requirement in a desperate effort to reduce the number of volunteers. It would thus have been counter-productive for the newly-formed PRC to launch an intensive poster campaign, and it is hardly surprising that at its first meeting the Publications Sub-Department cautiously agreed to issue nothing more elaborate than a simple Union Jack poster for announcing local meetings.[3]

Only at the start of October 1914, when it was clear that the War Office strategy was simply too effective, was the PRC asked to help restore the previous level of enlistment. On the instructions of the PRC General Purposes Committee the Publications Sub-Department thus began planning a systematic poster campaign, but the first of its designs, numbered PRC 1, still carried no more than the royal monogram and the words '"England Expects Every Man to do do His Duty" and Join the Army To-Day'. In November 1914 the Publications Sub-Department issued its first strip posters for trams and taxis, but these were equally plain, and the first of them, PRC 8, carried no more than the slogan 'A Call To Arms/ Your Country Needs You To-day'. The Sub-Department did not issue its first pictorial appeal, PRC 11, until later that month, and yet by the time that this poster appeared, with its smiling soldier and the words 'Follow Me! Your Country Needs You', more than a million men had already volunteered.[4]

The PRC continued to issue these new pictorial posters until September 1915, but during this period the trend of recruiting was steadily downwards. It is true that a million men volunteered during the main poster campaign, but it is dangerous to conclude from this that a single design such as Leete's 'Kitchener Wants You' had influenced their decision to enlist. Leete's portrait of

A display of recruiting posters at York station in 1915. The PRC particularly thanked 'railway and tramway companies' for their help with the poster campaign. Q 80627

Kitchener has featured in numerous books and articles about the war, but the persistent claim that it was 'the most famous and successful poster produced by the Parliamentary Recruiting Committee' has to be measured against the almost complete absence of contemporary references to it, either as the poster was first released or as it was later reissued by the printers David Allen and Sons, with the caption 'YOUR COUNTRY NEEDS YOU'. Indeed, if we look for references to Leete's design in the files of the PRC, or of the War Office, or of the Stationery Office, or in the published accounts of David Allen and Sons' wartime work, or in the newspapers and magazines which regularly criticised PRC posters, we find them conspicuous only by their absence.[5]

It seems that Leete's design made so little impact upon contemporaries that memories of Kitchener's face appearing 'on every hoarding' probably refer to another poster that was issued by the PRC in July 1915, showing the War Minister's impassive face beside the searching question 'DOES THE CALL OF DUTY FIND NO RESPONSE IN YOU UNTIL REINFORCED . . . BY THE CALL OF COMPULSION?'. This later design undoubtedly played an important part in the official campaign, for it was issued in two different sizes, numbered PRC 113 and 117, and within a few weeks David Allen and Sons had printed some 145,000 copies, making it undoubtedly the most numerous of all the PRC posters. Known officially as 'the "Lord Kitchener" poster', it was considered sufficiently important for a copy to be hung in the PRC's Downing Street office, and for its production to be mentioned in the official summary of the committee's work, neither of these honours being given to Alfred Leete's earlier Kitchener poster.[6]

There are similar problems in proving that Savile Lumley's 'Daddy, what did YOU do in the Great War?' had any significance in the recruiting campaign. Lumley's poster was first issued in March 1915 as PRC 79, but it was just one of fourteen new PRC designs released that month, and was not considered sufficiently distinctive to be noted either in the national newspapers or in the advertising and billposting journals. It was not among the nineteen PRC designs reproduced in a long article on 'Recruiting by Poster' in the *Windsor Magazine* of June 1915, nor was it one of the twelve PRC posters selected by WD and HO Wills for reproduction as a cigarette card in August 1915, nor one of the many PRC designs singled out for parody by newspaper cartoonists. 'Daddy, what did YOU do in the Great War?' was not even among the top fifteen PRC posters in terms of the numbers produced, and, as with Leete's Kitchener design, anyone wishing to prove its contemporary importance is facing considerable problems.[7]

Of course, the lack of contemporary impact does not lessen the value of these designs as evidence of the government's attempt to manipulate opinion. However, it has to be understood that the recruiting posters which did impress contemporaries were of a quite different type. The evidence comes mainly from the number of copies of each poster that were printed by the PRC, for although this largely indicates their popularity with recruiting officers it also indirectly reveals their impact on potential recruits. As the trade journal the *Billposter* observed in 1915, 'part of the testimony as to the efficacy of the posters comes from the soldiers themselves, who in large numbers have told the recruiting agent which particular poster has done the work in their own especial case.' Some new recruits even claimed

The most popular of all the PRC poster designs, of which David Allen and Sons printed 145,000 copies in July 1915. Known officially as 'the "Lord Kitchener" poster', it was issued in two sizes, numbered PRC 113 and 117. Department of Art, 0309

The eleven PRC poster designs which W D and H O Wills released as cigarette cards in August 1915. They are versions of PRC 7, 11 and 12 from November 1914; PRC 16, from December 1914; PRC 37 from January 1915; PRC 20, 21 and 22 from December 1914; and PRC 34, 35 and 54 from January 1915. The last card is *RALLY ROUND THE FLAG*, produced for the Central London Recruiting Dept. Author's collection.

that 'a picture has appealed to them so affectingly that they avowedly "could not get it out of their head".'[8]

Such evidence convinced the authorities that the most effective designs were not those which bullied potential recruits, but rather those which projected 'a delightful geniality'. The posters in greatest demand thus included several which depicted smiling soldiers, such as PRC 11 of November 1914 captioned 'FOLLOW ME! YOUR COUNTRY NEEDS YOU', of which 55,000 were printed; PRC 22 of December 1914 headed 'COME ALONG, BOYS!' of which 92,000 were printed; and PRC 54 of January 1915 reading 'LINE UP, BOYS! ENLIST TO-DAY', of which 65,000 were printed. As the *Manchester Guardian* observed in March 1915, the posters on house walls and in shop windows gave a remarkably prosaic view of the conflict, for 'our men are seen going to war, not strung up rigidly and consciously for terrific deeds, but moving on in good humour and determination . . . One shows a soldier lighting his pipe on the march with the remark, "Arf a mo, Kaiser". Another shows three laughing Highland lads stepping out together. There are hardly any heroics.' In June 1915 the PRC acknowledged that these 'genial figure-designs' were still its most popular recruiting posters.[9]

Confirmation of this carefree tone came from the London campaign. London recruiting officers were certainly impressed by one poster addressed 'TO THE YOUNG WOMEN OF LONDON', which began with the pointed inquiry 'Is your "Best Boy" wearing Khaki? If not don't YOU THINK he should be?', but this was hardly characteristic of the overall campaign and was widely criticised. The Central London Recruiting Depot, which issued its own recruiting posters, admitted that the most successful of its designs were those based on PRC 63 'THE VETERAN'S FAREWELL', PRC 107 'OUR FLAG', and PRC 22 'COME ALONG BOYS'. The Depot's officials were indeed so impressed by the smiling soldier in this last PRC design that they added the slogan 'OUR CHEERY LADS NEED YOUR HELP'. The public response to such images was enormous, and when, in the summer of 1915, the London *Evening Standard* invited its readers to choose the best of the contemporary recruiting posters, it suggested PRC 54 'LINE UP, BOYS!', a picture of four highland soldiers on the march, 'their smooth and pink young faces alight with laughter and gay carelessness'.[10]

There is thus good reason to consider both 'KITCHENER WANTS YOU' and 'Daddy, what did YOU do in the Great War?' as quite unrepresentative of the general PRC campaign, and yet they would still have value as indicators of official opinion if we could prove that the government was actively involved in their production. Yet in the case of Leete's 'KITCHENER WANTS YOU' there is simply no evidence that it was in any sense an official design. Neither the original poster nor the David Allen and Sons reprint carries a PRC serial number or a Stationery Office imprint, and neither is referred to in the PRC minutes, listed in its poster catalogues, or included in the official summary of its work. Leete's 'KITCHENER WANTS YOU' is not to be found in any contemporary accounts of the PRC campaign, and was not one of the many posters proudly displayed on the walls of the PRC's Downing Street office. There is in fact no evidence that this design played any part in the official campaign, or was even regarded by contemporaries as an official poster.

There are in fact several reasons why Leete's design could not have been officially produced. Not only did it first appear in September 1914, when the PRC was still committed to letterpress posters, but it also employed a personal appeal that ran counter to the official tradition of recruiting in the name of the King. Several months earlier the War Office had made some concessions to modern methods by placing its newspaper publicity in the hands of a professional advertising expert named Hedley Le Bas, but his work was still closely directed, and when, on the outbreak of war, he was summoned to the War Office and ordered to design a wartime recruiting appeal, he was obliged to follow a very traditional pattern. Returning to his office Le Bas settled upon the patriotic heading 'YOUR KING AND COUNTRY NEED YOU', and left his assistant, Eric Field, to draw up the famous advertisement which appeared in national newspapers.[11]

Le Bas would personally have preferred a more individual style, and when Lord Kitchener was appointed Secretary of State for War he tried to shift the focus of his campaign away from the King and towards Lord Kitchener.

Lads, you're wanted. A popular design, issued in March 1915 as poster PRC 78, of which at least 65,000 copies were printed by David Allen and Sons. Q 33170

As he recalled, Kitchener 'was the only soldier with a great war name, won in the field, within the memory of the thousands of men the country wanted', and as a commercial advertiser Le Bas recognised 'the value of a good name'. Yet to his disappointment Kitchener would not allow his name to be used for anything more than a brief expression of confidence in the nation's patriotism, and not only insisted that the original heading should be preserved, but also that the concluding words 'JOIN THE ARMY TO-DAY!' should be replaced with the more traditional 'God Save the King'. This conservatism made it impossible for Le Bas to develop an effective recruiting campaign around Kitchener, and makes it very unlikely that Leete's 'Kitchener Wants You' could have gained the backing of the War Office in September 1914.[12]

The truth is that Leete's poster owed little either to the War Office or to the PRC. Alfred Leete was a professional cartoonist whose portrait of Kitchener was originally produced as an illustration for *London Opinion*, a small-circulation magazine which characterised itself as 'a topical, literary, humourous, illustrated weekly journal'. The illustration was probably completed at the end of August 1914, and originally featured a portrait of Lord Kitchener over the caption 'Your Country Needs You', which was obviously intended as a reference to Le Bas's newspaper campaign. Leete's portrait of Kitchener, which he drew in an uncharacteristically sober style, was used on the cover of the issue for 5 September 1914, but it is unlikely that many people saw it in this form, for *London Opinion* was not a great success, and its owner admitted that 'circulation slumped horribly in the first weeks of the war'.[13]

The poster which was developed from Leete's drawing was a wholly private venture, and in December 1914 the magazine's editor referred to it quite plainly as 'the famous Kitchener recruiting poster, issued by LONDON OPINION'. This was not the only example of a private recruiting appeal, for the *London Opinion's* action was matched by James Crossley Eno, the manufacturer of Eno's Fruit Salt, who had already purchased a painting by Frank Dadd called *Follow the Drum* and had successfully transformed it into a recruiting poster. An even closer parallel came from Lord Northcliffe's *Weekly Dispatch*, which in November 1914 had carried a photo-montage of a wounded soldier on the battlefield, with an inset of a football crowd and the caption 'Will They Never Come?'. Northcliffe's Associated Newspapers reproduced this design as a recruiting poster, and issued it free to cinemas in the form of a lantern-slide, leading the War Office to congratulate Northcliffe on 'a brilliant contribution to the recruiting campaign'.[14]

***EVERYONE SHOULD DO HIS BIT*, issued as PRC 121 in August 1915 and printed by Roberts and Leete. The Stationery Office described it as showing 'some familiar posters', prominent among which are PRC 22 *COME ALONG, BOYS!* from December 1914 and PRC 54 *LINE UP, BOYS!* from January 1915, which the PRC issued as 'a companion poster to No. 22'. Department of Art, 5060**

Thus, far from revealing the government's methods, the appearance of Leete's 'Kitchener Wants You' on London hoardings in September and October 1914 was a purely private venture that ran counter to official policy. Lord Kitchener would certainly not have authorised this use of his image, and if the War Office was drawn into the *London Opinion* recruiting campaign it can only have been to the extent of agreeing to display this poster on official hoardings or at London recruiting stations. This may seem remarkable, but we can trace the same private inspiration behind Lumley's 'Daddy, what did YOU do in the Great War?', for although the PRC was eventually responsible for printing and distributing this recruiting poster, there is no evidence that government officials were involved either in its planning or in its design.

The basic idea can once again be traced back to Hedley Le Bas. In November 1914 the War Office finally agreed to sanction a more commercial newspaper campaign, and Le Bas gathered a number of like-minded advertising men into an unofficial Voluntary Recruiting Publicity Committee. As one advertiser recalled, 'this committee met once a week for consultation at York House,

St. James's Palace ... and they served without compensation of any kind'. 'Each advertisement they prepared in consultation was carefully written and criticised, and was submitted by Mr. Le Bas for the approval of the Army Council as the combined result of seven men's efforts to give the best of their knowledge for the country's good'. The committee included well-known advertising experts such as Wareham Smith of the *Daily Mail*, Henry Simonis of the *Daily News*, John Ackerman of the *Times*, and Thomas Russell, a prominent advertising consultant. Working outside government control, and using newspaper space donated by patriotic proprietors, these men managed to transform the recruiting appeal into a fully-fledged press campaign.[15]

In January 1915, as part of this new campaign, the members of the Voluntary Recruiting Publicity Committee issued a newspaper advertisement headed '5 Questions to men who have not enlisted', which sought to twist the arms of reluctant civilians. This style of advertisement caught the imagination of the authorities, and was almost immediately reprinted by the PRC Publications Sub-Department as Leaflet No. 29, in a run of 100,000 copies. Recruiting officers told Le Bas that, in combination with subsequent advertisements headed '4 Questions to the Women of England' and '5 Questions to those who employ male servants', this newspaper appeal proved enormously effective in bringing volunteers. Yet the War Office was still alarmed by its bullying tone. As Le Bas admitted, Lord Kitchener was 'startled' by this new and forceful style of recruiting, and remained 'a little suspicious about the popular appeals that departed so drastically from traditions he had respected all his life'.[16]

The fourth of the Voluntary Recruiting Publicity Committee's '5 Questions to men who have not enlisted' asked 'What will you answer when your children grow up, and say, "Father, why weren't you a soldier too?"'. Thomas Russell later claimed to have been 'mainly responsible' for this particular advertisement, but, whatever its origins, the idea of a patriotic child challenging its father immediately caught the imagination of the committee. As Le Bas recalled: 'I was rather taken with the possibilities of that question ... and took it down to Sir Owen Seaman, of *Punch*, to see if a cartoon could be based on it. It was Bernard Partridge, I think, who drew one. The time was supposed to be about 1930, and the picture showed a little boy asking his father what he did in the great war. For the purpose of the cartoon, the cartoonist added the word "Daddy".'[17]

In February 1915 Partridge's cartoon was duly released as an unofficial recruiting leaflet, showing a man at home reading a newspaper and being surprised by his young son demanding to know 'DADDY, WHY WEREN'T YOU A SOLDIER DURING THE WAR?' The text below this picture warned the reader that 'IN YEARS TO COME YOU MAY BE ASKED THIS QUESTION. Join the Army at once, and help to secure the glorious Empire of which your little son will be a citizen'. However, this was not the final version of this heart-rending appeal, for in January 1915 the question had surfaced again in PRC 57, David Allen and Sons' poster version of the Voluntary Recruiting Publicity Committee's '5 QUESTIONS TO MEN WHO HAVE NOT ENLISTED'. In the following month Chorley and Pickersgill produced yet another version for the PRC, which showed a boy scout and his father in black silhouette, with the text 'WHAT WILL YOUR ANSWER BE/ When your boy asks you-/ "FATHER — WHAT DID YOU DO TO HELP WHEN BRITAIN FOUGHT FOR FREEDOM IN 1915?"'.[18]

The Chorley and Pickersgill design was issued as poster number PRC 61, but whilst it was obviously inspired by the previous recruiting appeals on this theme it was still not the last to appear. In March 1915 Arthur Gunn, a director of the poster printers Johnson, Riddle and Company, decided to employ the question as the basis for yet another recruiting design. Transforming the boy into a little girl, he instructed his poster artist Savile Lumley to redraw Partridge's cartoon as a domestic scene set about five years in the future, with the slightly amended slogan 'Daddy, what did YOU do in the Great War?'. When the design was finished Gunn took it along to the PRC offices in Downing Street to obtain the approval of the Publications Sub-Department, and duly returned with a commission to print it as poster number PRC 79.[19]

The production of this design was thus the work of Thomas Russell, a professional advertiser; Hedley Le Bas, a mail-order publisher; Bernard Partridge, a professional cartoonist; Arthur Gunn, a poster printer; and Savile Lumley, a commercial artist. None of them was employed by the government, and the only official involvement in the production of PRC 79 came in its final approval by the Publications Sub-Department. Yet the Sub-Department was no more than Humphrey Davies, private secretary to the Liberal Chief Whip, and Malcolm Fraser, head of the Conservative Party Publication Department, who were so inexperienced that they happily agreed to whatever suggestions the trade put forward. When Gunn came away from their offices it was with a commission to print PRC 79 not only according to his own design and on his own machines, but also using a rather expensive process of eight separate colour printings.[20]

This was the pattern for the entire PRC poster campaign. At least thirty-six different printing companies were involved in printing the numbered designs, but it is

WHAT WILL YOUR ANSWER BE? **issued as poster PRC 61 in February 1915 and printed by Chorley and Pickersgill. Department of Art: POS 243**

The office of the PRC Publications Sub-Department at 11 Downing Street, shown at the close of the poster campaign in 1915. Savile Lumley's *Daddy, what did YOU do in the Great War?* hangs on the wall by the light. BL ADD 54192 By permission of the British Library.

notable that only a handful of them were printed by more than one firm at a time. The vast majority were apparently designed and printed by the same company, and the PRC campaign was heavily influenced by those large firms which ran their own design departments. About half of all the PRC poster designs were in fact printed either by David Allen and Sons, or by Roberts and Leete, Chorley and Pickersgill, Hazell, Watson and Viney, or Johnson, Riddle, and Company, and the likelihood is that they were also designed within these five companies. At the close of the campaign it was indeed admitted that David Allen and Sons had printed 1,500,000 copies of 40 different posters, 'the majority of which were designed in their own works'. This pattern is hardly surprising, for it was the way that the commercial poster industry normally worked.[21]

The truth is that posters such as 'KITCHENER WANTS YOU' and 'Daddy, what did YOU do in the Great War?' did not reflect the attitudes of government, but rather those of a new breed of commercial advertisers and graphic designers whose involvement in the recruiting campaign was widely resented. The rapid growth of a national market for cheap branded goods had brought these advertising experts into prominence, but their rising status inevitably brought them into conflict with the upper and middle classes, whose dominance of consumer retailing they were helping to undermine. The bold techniques which they brought to consumer advertising were widely condemned, and when it was suggested that the same methods might be adopted by national politicians this resistance rapidly increased. In March 1912 there had been alarm when the advertising expert Charles Higham inserted 'A Personal Word to the Chief Party Whips' in the advertising columns of the London morning papers, urging the major political parties to behave 'as the great national advertisers of this country do—explaining the merits of the proposition as a manufacturer of a household commodity presents his—simply, clearly, and convincingly'.[22]

As Higham insisted, it seemed to him 'as easy to create votes as it is to change the breakfast food of a nation', and although nothing came of his bold venture, the development of full-scale political campaigns was still one of the long-term goals of the British advertising industry. Advertising experts were confident that they could teach the public about politics 'in the same way as they taught them about Colman's mustard', and they urged the party managers to 'make use of the regular advertising columns . . . use the personal letter, apply the principles of the "follow-up", make more intelligent use of posters, and, in fact, conduct a campaign on just the same lines as Rowntree's, Scott's Emulsion, the Underground Railway, and other commercial enterprises'. Advertisers believed that the time had come for national politicians to abandon their traditional restraint and address the public in the language of the mass market. Similar tactics were advocated for central government, and in 1913 the War Office was urged to adopt 'real, "live," modern methods', and to swell the ranks of the Army and Territorial Force with bold advertisements headed 'YOUNG MAN,/ Your Country Calls You' and 'EMPLOYERS,/ Here's a Straight Talk with You'.[23]

Even before Le Bas began his wartime campaign British advertising experts had thus made an effort to modernise the political process, but they had also begun to encounter considerable resistance from those who believed that modern advertising had no part to play in a democratic campaign. On the outbreak of war British advertising experts thus urged the War Office to issue recruiting posters 'that would "sell the goods",' but the prospect of exchanging the traditional style of government

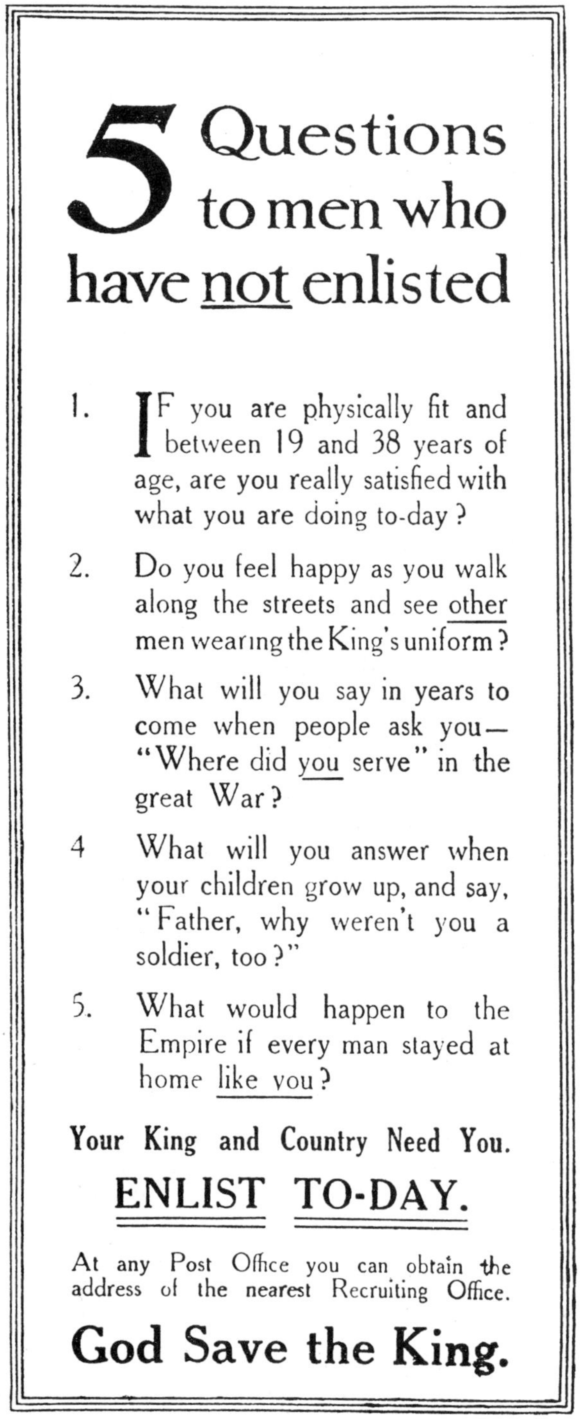

5 Questions to men who have not enlisted

1. IF you are physically fit and between 19 and 38 years of age, are you really satisfied with what you are doing to-day ?

2. Do you feel happy as you walk along the streets and see other men wearing the King's uniform ?

3. What will you say in years to come when people ask you—"Where did you serve" in the great War ?

4 What will you answer when your children grow up, and say, "Father, why weren't you a soldier, too ?"

5. What would happen to the Empire if every man stayed at home like you ?

Your King and Country Need You.

ENLIST TO-DAY.

At any Post Office you can obtain the address of the nearest Recruiting Office.

God Save the King.

The Voluntary Recruiting Publicity Committee's *5 Questions to men who have not enlisted,* which Le Bas placed in London newspapers on 4 January 1915. H Le Bas, *The Lord Kitchener Memorial Book,* London, 1916.

for the brash commercialism of the mass market was anathema to both politicians and civil servants, and there was widespread concern that a professional advertiser like Le Bas should be permitted to direct an official campaign. In August 1914 his dignified newspaper appeals were thus criticised simply for appearing in the advertising columns, where it was said that patriotic readers had been astonished to find 'an appeal to the nation to risk its life and an appeal to the public to drink only So-and-So's wine-tonic, cheek by jowl'.[24]

As the recruiting campaign developed these links between official publicity and commercial advertising became even stronger. Le Bas liked to describe his newspaper recruiting campaign as 'advertising for an army', and in January 1915 the Publicity Committee's '5 Questions to men who have not enlisted' could be seen to bear an uncomfortable resemblance to a well-known newspaper advertisement headed 'Seven Convincing Reasons Why you Should secure a PIANOLA PIANO'. This commercialisation was not confined to the Voluntary Recruiting Publicity Committee, for in February 1915 the PRC Publications Sub-Department not only converted a tobacco advertisement into poster PRC 63, but even added the acknowledgment 'REPRODUCED BY KIND PERMISSION OF MESSRS. ABDULLA & CO. LTD'. There could be no plainer admission that the government was using the techniques of the mass market, and the *Daily Mail* revelled in this demonstration 'that given patriotic impulse advertising for people to go to a war is just like advertising for people to buy a popular cigarette or a new boot polish'.[25]

By April 1915 the official recruiting posters were largely indistinguishable from contemporary advertisements. Poster companies such as David Allen and Sons, which submitted dozens of designs to the PRC Publications Sub-Department, freely mixed the official imagery with the consumer advertising they continued to produce for private clients. No one who saw their poster of smiling soldiers and sailors with pens the size of rifles and the caption 'YOU'LL HEAR FROM US — WE'VE GOT "SWAN" PENS', could fail to see the similarity. By September 1915 the two styles of publicity were indeed so interlinked that the *Bystander* magazine could produce a page of cartoons headed 'What to Do With Our War Posters', showing how easily the recruiting appeals could be turned into commercial advertisements 'if the war were to end suddenly'. As they demonstrated, it was ludicrously simple to change a design like PRC 96 of May 1915, with a smiling soldier and the caption 'HE'S HAPPY AND SATISFIED', into an advertisement for a restaurant just by adding the slogan 'HE'S HAD LUNCH AT PHILLEM'S CORNER HOUSE'.[26]

The PRC Publications Sub-Department was

happy to accept the advice of commercial advertisers, but the problem for the government was that by using such 'frankly commercial' images it managed to alienate both the supporters of voluntary enlistment and those who favoured some form of conscription. The Liberal government's traditional supporters thus argued that such blatant commercialism was contrary to the whole spirit of voluntary enlistment, complaining that the PRC was obviously seeking sensation, and that a simple arrow with the words 'To the Recruiting Office' was 'the only right and dignified poster which should ever be seen on walls or hoardings'. Yet at the same time the Conservative supporters of conscription took the growing commercialism of the poster campaign as further evidence that the voluntary system had failed, and claimed that despite its obvious cleverness the PRC's frantic attempt to raise recruits was 'a humiliating confession of the Government's reluctance to face facts'.[27]

As the war continued the blatant commercialism of the official poster campaign thus provoked considerable and growing opposition. The PRC designs were simply too reminiscent of consumer advertising, and, as one critic observed in June 1915, 'a method which might have been unexceptional for calling attention to the virtues of a shop, a soap, a circus, or a pill, seemed inappropriate in the case of a great nation struggling at the crisis of its fate'. The language of the mass market was regarded as wholly inappropriate to the raising of a national army, and critics attacked the organisation of the official recruiting campaign as a cowardly surrender to commercial ideology. 'The grand mistake made by the War Office', observed one writer in September 1915, 'was in putting the matter in the hands of persons who looked on recruiting as something to be pushed in the same manner as pills or soap'.[28]

Some critics even argued that the commercialism of the official campaign had prevented men from enlisting, and that 'for every recruit drawn to the ranks . . . ten have been disgusted and driven away'. One recruiting officer claimed that the PRC's poster campaign was especially counter-productive, noting that by 1915 the War Office was trying to reach a section of the working class that was 'sub-cynical, undemonstrative, and irresponsive to cheap rhetoric', and that this form of publicity simply failed to catch its attention: 'The pictorial poster, with the figure of Nelson under the caption "England expects every man to do his Duty"; or of the widow resigning her claims on her young son and bidding him go to the wars; or of the draped Union Jack, left it cold; and if any remark was elicited that remark was probably some cheap witless gibe'. By 1915 many people had similar doubts, and although advertising

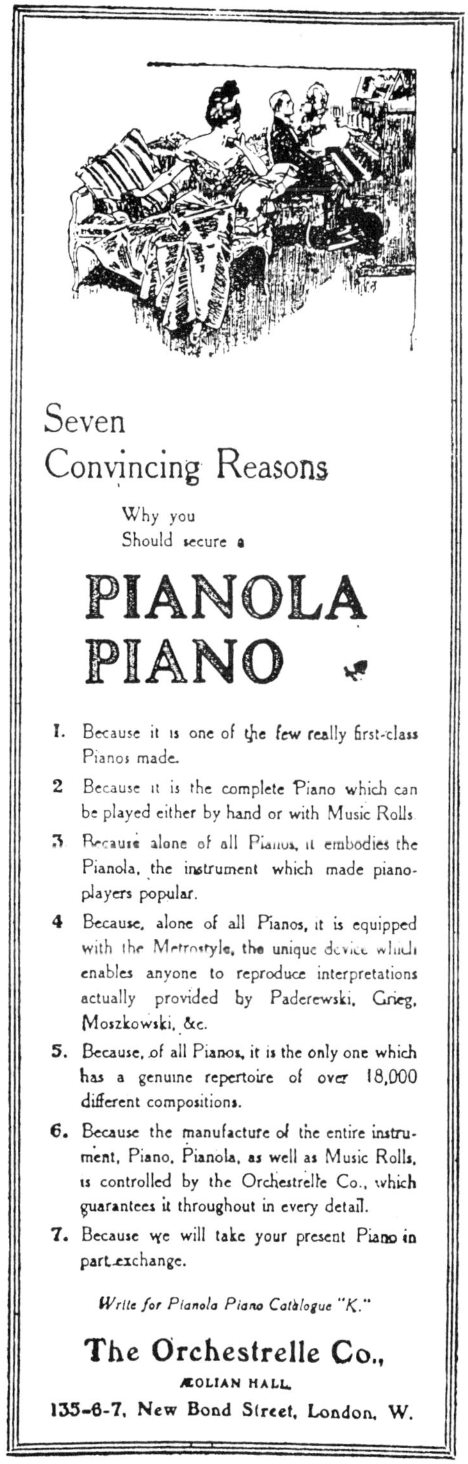

There is an obvious similarity between the Voluntary recruiting Publicity Committee's *5 Questions to men who have not enlisted* and the pre-war advertisement *Seven Convincing Reasons Why you Should secure a PIANOLA PIANO*, which was praised in one of Le Bas's own publications as a design which 'really attracts the eye and invites attention'. W S M Knight, *The Business Encyclopaedia and Legal Advertiser*, London, 1907, vol VII, p 243.

***THE VETERAN'S FAREWELL*, a tobacco advertisement which was adapted as poster PRC 24 in December 1914, and was reissued in full colour as PRC 63 in February 1915. The PRC Considered it 'a fine appeal to the manhood of the nation', and printed 71,500 copies. Department of Art, 2666**

experts might claim success for these modern methods, the man in the street was said to regard the PRC poster campaign with increasing distaste, for 'it bored him and he was disposed to resent it'.[29]

By June 1915 it was indeed being argued that the working classes 'regarded the whole of this "publicity" campaign with distrust and dislike', and that they 'resented the hints and instructions which were so obligingly given by the "publicity artists" and the "party managers" to the well-to-do classes—to employers of all sorts—as to how they should bring pressure to bear upon their dependents'. There was some solid basis for this resentment, for in July 1915 the managers of one company assured the PRC that 'we are much obliged to you for the posters you sent . . . and they appear to have achieved the object we had in view, for several of our people whom we could very well dispense with have entered the Service'. Many critics condemned the PRC campaign as 'bullying by poster', and questions such as 'Daddy, what did YOU do in the Great War?' eventually aroused as much resentment as they did patriotic enthusiasm. Robert Smillie, the Scottish miners' leader, claimed that his answer would be 'I tried to stop the bloody thing, my child'.[30]

In fact the British public was gradually alienated by the PRC campaign. By the end of April 1915 the Stationery Office had printed well over three million individual posters for the Publications Sub-Department, and over the next five months it added an average of 600,000 posters a month to this massive total. Most of these were the full-colour designs that historians have considered virtually irresistible, but the cold statistics tell a different story. As the enlistment rate fell from 135,000 in May 1915, to 115,000 in June, and finally to 95,000 in July, it was apparent that almost six PRC posters were needed to bring forward a single volunteer. This level of response would not have satisfied a commercial advertiser, and the tide of government opinion began to turn against a poster campaign which now seemed both wasteful and uneconomic. By the end of July 1915 confidence in the official campaign had indeed fallen to such a low ebb that the War Office begged the PRC to suspend its operations, arguing that its target audience was now clearly 'sick of posters and recruiting meetings'.[31]

As public enthusiasm declined it seems that the PRC Publications Sub-Department also encountered problems in distributing its posters. In the first months of the campaign people were happy to display the recruiting posters on walls and hoardings, and by the beginning of January 1915 an average of 30,000 copies had been distributed of each of thirty-two numbered designs. The Publications Sub-Department continued to release new designs at an impressive rate, and by the end of March 1915 it had issued another fifty numbered posters. However, it seems that the market had been saturated, for demand had dropped so far that only 20,000 copies of each new poster had been sent out. The Stationery Office continued to print large numbers of new PRC designs, but they proved increasingly difficult to place with the public. By the end of June 1915 the Publications Sub-Department had released another twenty-nine numbered designs, but the figures suggest that only 17,000 copies of each new poster had been distributed.[32]

The result was a growing stockpile of undistributed posters. By the end of March 1915 the Publications Sub-Department had circulated some 2 million posters, but it still had copies of thirty-nine different designs dating back to the start of the campaign, and begged for help from 'builders, property-owners, and others who have vacant hoardings or wall space'. Distribution was clearly falling well behind production, and although the Stationery Office had already printed more than 3 million recruiting posters by the end of April 1915, there were still only 2.5 million of them in circulation two months later. By July 1915, when the Publications

What to Do with Our War Posters

A HINT TO ADVERTISERS

Showing how, if the war were to end suddenly, the surplus stock of recruiting posters left on the country's hands could be usefully turned to account

A series of parodies by Alick Ritchie, from *The Bystander* of 8 September 1915, proving how easily the PRC campaign could be returned to its commercial origins. LD 50 The Bystander 08.09.1915. By permission of the British Library.

***COME AND DO YOUR BIT!* and *HE'S HAPPY AND SATISFIED*, issued as posters PRC 93 and 96 in April 1915, and *GO! IT'S YOUR DUTY LAD*, issued as poster PRC 109 in June 1915. The Stationery Office called the last design 'a well executed poster illustrating the indomitable spirit of the Mothers of Britain', but *The Bystander* showed how these posters all had their roots in consumer advertising. Q 79994, Q 80140, Q 70864**

Sub-Department was forced to suspended its poster production, there may have been as many as a million undistributed posters and show cards in store, strengthening the War Office claim that the campaign had become a 'waste of money'. In an effort to reduce its stockpile the Publications Sub-Department began to send large numbers of posters overseas to reinforce the imperial recruiting campaign, and 'many tons' were eventually disposed of to Canada, Newfoundland, British Columbia, India, Australia, New Zealand, and South Africa.[33]

The suspension of PRC poster production in July 1915 marked a turning point in official attitudes to the recruiting campaign. During August 1915 the Publications Sub-Department released only four new poster designs, its lowest monthly output since the campaign began. In the middle of September 1915 it was allowed to restart its poster production, but there were now considerable doubts as to the practical value of such a discredited campaign. Charles Masterman, the government's director of propaganda in neutral countries, argued quite openly that the PRC's methods had not influenced enlistment rates by more than a few percent, for 'the so-called "pressure" of voluntaryism ... has scarcely counted amongst the great massed sections of population which make up the bulk of the new Armies'. The arguments for commercial publicity no longer carried much weight in government, for by September 1915 recruiting had slumped to 72,000 men a month, despite the fact that, as one contemporary observed, 'posters and placards calling for volunteers were more abundant, more artistic, and more persuasive than ever'.[34]

By the end of September 1915 official confidence in the poster campaign had in fact evaporated. When Lord Derby was appointed Director-General of Recruiting at the start of October 1915 he had no hesitation in declaring 'that pictorial posters had had their day', and quickly purged his department of all the trappings of consumer advertising. The Publications Sub-Department was instructed to cancel all but the few illustrated posters which still remained in the press, and Lord Derby ensured that the official recruiting appeal would in future return to its nineteenth-century origins. PRC 133 of September 1915 was thus a striking full-colour poster of a cavalryman charging at the observer, with the words 'Forward to Victory / ENLIST NOW', but under Lord Derby's guidance PRC 134 of November 1915 became a simple black letterpress notice with the blunt heading 'SINGLE MEN FIRST / HOW THE GROUP SYSTEM WORKS'.[35]

There are thus considerable problems in regarding the PRC poster campaign of 1914 and 1915 as a turning point in official propaganda. As we have seen, almost a million men had enlisted before the Publications Sub-Department decided to issue its first pictorial poster, and its main campaign was only allowed to run for nine months before the War Office intervened to prevent any further 'waste of money'. The poster campaign was then allowed to restart, but it was subsequently cancelled in the middle of the worst recruiting crisis the country had yet seen, with few people to mourn its passing. By October 1915 even the advertising profession had turned against the recruiting posters, and whilst the *Placard* attacked the PRC for failing to run a centralised campaign, the *Advertising World* surveyed the acres of tattered posters and declared that it was 'impossible . . . to avoid reflecting upon the prodigious waste of effort and money represented by them'.[36]

Historians must therefore approach images such as Alfred Leete's 'KITCHENER WANTS YOU' and Savile Lumley's 'Daddy, what did YOU do in the Great War?' with considerable caution, for despite their notoriety they do not give direct access to the emotions that swept Britain during 1914 and 1915. The evidence suggests that in fact the majority of the population was gradually alienated by the growing commercialism of the poster campaign, and that the status of these images as icons of the war is based not upon their first use in the recruiting campaign, but on the later ironic use of their slogans as popular catchphrases. By 1915 British soldiers were already using the catchphrase 'KITCHENER WANTS YOU' whenever anyone was selected for an especially filthy job or a particularly dangerous duty, and this was not the only such adaptation from the recruiting campaign. The slogan 'REMEMBER BELGIUM', which appeared on 140,000 copies of PRC 16 and PRC 19, was also used by soldiers with bitter irony, often attracting the reply 'As if I'm ever likely to forget the place!'[37]

The only contemporary references to Lumley's poster are similarly anti-heroic, deriving their power from the ironic contrast between the heightened emotions of the PRC poster campaign and the reality of life in the army. In 1915 the postcard designer Donald McGill produced a version of PRC 79 in which the slogan 'DADDY, WHAT DID YOU DO IN THE GREAT WAR?' appeared as the caption to a picture of a sweating soldier on kitchen duty. In March 1916 a similar parody appeared in the trench magazine of the Lancashire Fusiliers, in the shape of a poem that began 'What did you do in the Great War, Dad?/ Please Daddy, tell us, do;/ For they censor all your letters,/ So we know they can't be true'. In May 1916 there was a further ironic reference to the poster, when the Winner Record Company released a recording of Stanley Kirkby singing 'What Did You Do in the Great War, Daddy?' As the title indicates, it

The origins of Leete's *KITCHENER WANTS YOU* did not lie in official announcements, but in prewar consumer advertising, as this poster for BDV Cigarettes demonstrates. H Bridgewater, *Advertising or the Art of Making Known*, London, 1910, p 15.

SOME RECRUITING FROM THE ARMY POSTERS
Hints for the Peace Office when the time comes for recruiting for Civilian Ranks

Parodies published in *The Bystander* of 25 August 1915, showing how the recruiting campaign might be adapted 'should the normal conditions of war be rudely disturbed by an outbreak of European Peace'. Included is a parody by Alick Ritchie of Leete's *KITCHENER WANTS YOU.* LD 50 The Bystander 25.08.1915. By permission of the British Library.

was a response to the catchphrase rather than to the original poster. By 1917 the expression 'What Did You Do in the Great War, Daddy?' was being used by British soldiers at the front in times of distress and misery, and, according to one account, it often produced the laconic response 'Shut up, you little bastard! Get the Bluebell and go and clean my medals'.[38]

The recruiting poster campaign was thus not quite as has been presented. It is true that coercive and manipulative images were produced to encourage enlistment during 1914 and 1915, and an attempt was made to bully and shame men into joining the army. Some of these designs, such as Alfred Leete's 'Kitchener Wants You' and Savile Lumley's 'Daddy, what did YOU do in the Great War?', became so notorious that their slogans passed into common currency. However, such posters were very unusual, and must be approached with caution. They give little insight into the process of voluntary enlistment, for they were uncharacteristic of the general poster campaign, and cannot give access to the official mind, for their inspiration was largely unofficial. If they demonstrate anything it is the attitude of commercial publicists to the problems of democratic government, and the judgement of contemporaries seems to have been close to that of later generations: amazement, disbelief, and disgust by turns, hardening into an ironic detachment that manifested itself in jokes and parodies.

It was indeed these ironic references to Leete and Lumley's designs which formed the basis of their postwar notoriety, and the closer one looks at the history of these very commercial images the more it appears that their lasting fame dates from the 1920s and 1930s, when many people wished to see the war as having been forced upon a peaceful nation by a subtle and manipulative government. It was in these years that the Stationery Office brought new prominence to Lumley's design by selling off the remaining stock of PRC posters, for it still possessed copies of eighty-one different designs and blithely offered these to libraries and museums as 'a unique opportunity . . . of acquiring sets or individual copies of the numerous pictorial posters . . . which figured so prominently upon the hoardings'. The Imperial War Museum played a similar role in popularising Leete's design, for it had obtained his original drawing and now supplied so many copies for publication that even old soldiers began to believe that the original poster had carried the slogan 'YOUR COUNTRY NEEDS YOU'.[39]

The conclusion must be that recruiting posters such as Leete's 'KITCHENER WANTS YOU' and Lumley's 'Daddy, what did YOU do in the Great War?' are famous because we want them to be famous, not because they give us access to the dominant emotions of the recruiting campaign. Many people still wish to see 1914 and 1915 as the time when a pacific nation fell under the control of a belligerent state, but, as we have seen, the truth is far more complex. Far from being a monolithic official campaign, many recruiting posters had entirely private origins, whilst even those which belonged to the PRC campaign were largely designed not by government officials but by commercial advertisers and graphic designers who were eager to show their patriotism. In a similar way the recruiting campaign met with a mixed response from the public, and although it gained much of its impact by adopting the imagery of the mass market, this also proved to be the source of its greatest weakness. By 1914 the British public was already skilled in resisting the power of commercial advertising, and it simply transferred to the recruiting campaign that ironic detachment which had developed from years of exposure to the inflated claims of products such as Rowntree's Cocoa, Pears' Soap, and Colman's Mustard.

***TAKE UP THE SWORD OF JUSTICE*, a poster recalling the sinking of the *Lusitania* in May 1915. Drawn by Bernard Partridge of *Punch*, it was one of the few designs actually commissioned by the PRC, which ordered 105,000 copies from David Allen and Sons in June 1915, issuing it in three sizes as posters PRC 105, 106 and 111. Department of Art, 0409**

Appendix A:
The output of PRC Designs.

The main sequence of PRC posters was consecutively numbered, with the numbers apparently being issued in chronological order. The list below gives the approximate monthly output of PRC poster designs, derived from the imprints on surviving posters and based on the highest-numbered design known to have been issued in each month.

Month:	Designs issued:	Month's output:
October 1914	PRC 1–5	5
November 1914	PRC 6–15	10
December 1914	PRC 16–32	17
January 1915	PRC 33–57	25
February 1915	PRC 58–68	11
March 1915	PRC 69–82	14
April 1915	PRC 83–97	15
May 1915	PRC 98–104	7
June 1915	PRC 105–111	7
July 1915	PRC 112–119	8
August 1915	PRC 120–123	4
September 1915	PRC 124–133	10

Appendix B:
The most popular designs in the PRC Poster campaign.

In 1916 the PRC Publications Sub-Department revealed which had been the 'most popular' poster designs in terms of the total number printed. This list can be supplemented with other information gathered from surviving posters, to give the fifteen 'most popular' PRC designs, all of which were produced in runs totalling 50,000 copies or more. The companies which printed these different designs are also given.[40]

All PRC posters carry a Stationery Office imprint, giving the Warrant number, the print run, and the date of printing. 'W.12400 10M 2/15' thus indicates that in February 1915 the Stationery Office ordered 10,000 copies of this design, which was identified as job number 12400. The entire printing history of a poster can sometimes be determined in this way. The PRC report thus shows that 65,000 copies of 'Line Up Boys! Enlist Today' were printed, and surviving copies reveal that this was made up of 25,000 printed in January 1915, 20,000 in March 1915, and 20,000 in April 1915.[41]

1. ['The "Lord Kitchener" Poster']
   Photograph of Lord Kitchener with text from speech, including: 'DOES THE CALL OF DUTY FIND NO RESPONSE IN YOU UNTIL REINFORCED . . . BY THE CALL OF COMPULSION?'
   145,000 copies.
   Printed by David Allen and Sons, c.July-August 1915, as posters PRC 113 (30″ x 20″) and 117 (50″ x 40″).
2. 'REMEMBER BELGIUM ENLIST TODAY'
   In the official description, 'a British soldier on guard in the foreground whilst in the background a woman and her babes are in flight from a blazing home'.
   140,000 copies.
   Designed and printed by Henry Jenkinson Ltd, c.December-March 1915, as posters PRC 16 (40″ x 30″) and 19 (20″ x 15″).
3. 'TAKE UP THE SWORD OF JUSTICE'
   The sinking of the *Lusitania*, with a figure rising from the sea and offering a sword.
   105,000 copies.
   Commissioned by the PRC from Bernard Partridge of Punch. Printed by David Allen and Sons, c.June 1915, as posters PRC 105 (40″ x 25″), 106 (60″ x 40″), and 111 (30″ x 20″).
4. 'We're both needed to serve the Guns! FILL UP THE RANKS! PILE UP THE MUNITIONS!'
   A soldier and munition worker shaking hands, with a battle scene in the background.
   101,000 copies.

We're both needed to serve the Guns! **Another of the PRC's rare commissions, apparently produced at the request of the War Office in May 1915. The PRC ordered some 101,000 copies from Chorley and Pickersgill, issuing it in three sizes as posters PRC 85A, 85B and 85C. Department of Art, 5112**

Commissioned by the PRC, apparently at the request of the War Office, and printed by Chorley and Pickersgill Ltd, c.May 1915, as posters PRC 85A (probably 120″ x 80″), 85B (50″ x 40″), and 85C (30″ x 20″).

5. 'He did his duty. Will YOU do YOURS?'
   Portrait of Lord Roberts, with Victoria Cross and symbols of office.
   95,000 copies.
   Designed and printed by Johnson, Riddle and Co, c.December 1914, as poster PRC 20 (30″ x 20″). The company also printed a Welsh version, and used the same design in a poster for the Central London Recruiting Depot.
6. 'COME ALONG, BOYS! . . . ENLIST TODAY' ['The smiling soldier'.]
   A smiling soldier, with a quotation from Sir Horace Smith-Dorrien: 'The moment the order came to go forward, there were smiling faces everywhere'.
   92,000 copies.
   Designed by the Haycock-Cadle Co, and initially released c.November 1914 as the PRC's first 'window-card', PRC 100c (11″ x 11″). Also printed by the same company, c.December 1914—January 1915, as poster PRC 22 (30″ x 20″). The Haycock-Cadle Co also printed a Welsh version, and used its design in a poster for the Central London Recruiting Depot.
7. '"FALL IN" ANSWER NOW IN YOUR COUNTRY'S HOUR OF NEED'
   A bugler blowing a call.
   85,000 copies.
   Designed and printed by Hill, Siffken and Co, c.November 1914, as posters PRC 12 (30″ x 20″) and 13 (size unknown). The company also used its design in a large poster for the Central London Recruiting Depot.
8. 'THE VETERAN'S FAREWELL. "Good Bye, my lad, I only wish I were young enough to go with you!" ENLIST NOW!'
   A veteran shaking hands with a soldier, with new recruits in the background.
   71,500 copies.
   Initially designed by Frank Dadd of the *Graphic* as a tobacco advertisement. Subsequently used as a recruiting poster 'by Kind Permission of Messrs. Abdulla & Co. Ltd', and printed both by Straker Bros and by Petty and Sons, with a first release c. December 1914 and a reissue c.February 1915. Numbered PRC 24 (sepia 30″ x 20″—renumbered 63s on reissue), and 63 (full colour, 30″ x 20″).
9. 'LINE UP, BOYS! ENLIST TO-DAY'.
   Four kilted soldiers marching side by side.
   65,000 copies.
   Apparently designed by Eyre and Spottiswoode, who were described as 'owners of the copyright'. Printed by them and by A White and Co, January—April 1915, as poster PRC 54 (30″ x 20″).
10. 'Lads, you're wanted: GO AND HELP'.
    Advancing soldiers in silhouette.
    At least 65,000 copies.
    Printed by David Allen and Sons, c.March—May 1915, as poster PRC 78 (30″ x 6″).
11. 'ARE YOU DOING YOUR DUTY TODAY?'
    Lord Nelson and the sea, with heading '1805 "ENGLAND EXPECTS" 1915'.
    60,000 copies.
    Apparently designed by Seargeant Bros, who added 'Design Copyright' to the imprint. Printed by Seargeant Bros, c.May 1915, as poster PRC 101 (30″ x 20″), with the design later reused as a poster for the Publicity Department, Admiralty Recruiting Ofice.
12. 'If you cannot join the army – Try & get a Recruit'.
    White letterpress on red and blue background.
    At least 60,000 copies.
    Printed by the Haycock-Cadle Co, December—March 1915, as poster PRC 32 (30″ x 20″).
13. 'Follow me! YOUR COUNTRY NEEDS YOU"
    A marching soldier.
    55,000 copies.
    The picture is by 'E.K[eeley]', an artist who worked for Hill, Siffken and Co, the company which presumably designed the poster. Hill, Siffken and Co printed it c.November—December 1914 as poster PRC 11 (30″ x 20").
14. 'AT THE FRONT! Every fit Briton should join our brave men at the Front. ENLIST NOW'.
    Showing a field gun team amid shellbursts.
    55,000 copies.
    Printed by E S and A Robinson Ltd, c.April 1915, as poster PRC 84 (30″ x 20″).
15. 'BRITONS! YOUR COUNTRY NEEDS YOU'.
    Red lettering over grey map of Great Britain and Ireland.
    At least 50,000 copies.
    Printed by Saunders and Cullingham, in December 1914, as poster PRC 23 (30″ x 20″).

Notes

1. For the PRC and its poster campaign see R Douglas, 'Voluntary Enlistment in the First World War and the Parliamentary Recruiting Committee', *Journal of Modern History*, Vol 42, No.4, 1970, pp 564–585; J Darracott and B Loftus, *First World War Posters*, London, 1972, pp 5–12; B Curtis, 'Posters as Visual Propaganda in the First World War', *Block*, No. 2, Spring 1980, pp 45–57; and P Dutton, 'Moving images? The Parliamentary Recruiting Committee's poster campaign, 1914–1916', *Imperial War Museum Review*, No. 4, Imperial War Museum, London, 1989, pp 43–58. Leete's poster showed Kitchener's face over the slogan "WANTS YOU", but for convenience it will be referred to by its common title of 'KITCHENER WANTS YOU'.

2. J Allen, 'Men and Still More Men', *Placard*, January 1915, p 28; 'Recruiting by Poster', *Windsor Magazine*, June 1915, p 16; W J Avery, 'National Advertising in Posters', *Penrose's Annual 1916*, London, 1916, p 111; P[ublic] R[ecord] O[ffice, London], WO 106/367, 'Parliamentary Recruiting Committee: Publications Sub-Department Report', c. May 1916, p 3 and appendix 'Numbers and cost of publications'; C Sheldon, *Billposting: A practical handbook*, London, 1916, pp 31–32.

3. B[ritish] L[ibrary, London], Add. Mss. 54, 192, PRC Sub-Department Minutes, 3 September 1914, f.1; J E Edmonds (ed), *History of the Great War, Military Operations, France and Belgium 1915*, Vol I, HMSO, London, 1927, pp 50–51; M and E Brock(eds), *H H Asquith: Letters to Venetia Stanley*, Oxford University Press, Oxford, 1982, p 214 [2 September 1914].

4. BL, Add. Mss. 59, 192, PRC 'Minute Book No. 1', GPC meeting of 21 October 1914, ff. 4, 8; Sessional Papers 1921, 'General Annual Reports on the British Army . . . 1 October 1913 to 30 September 1919', HMSO, London, 1921, pp 6, 60. A large number of PRC posters can be dated from their Stationery Office imprints, and from contemporary references to their first appearance. The remainder can then be dated from their PRC numbers, which were issued in chronological order. For an approximate guide to dates see Appendix A.

5. J Darracott, *The First World War in Posters*, London, 1974, p xix; Avery, 'National Advertising in Posters', pp 110–112; W E D Allen, *David Allens: The history of a family firm 1857–1957*, London, 1957, pp 218–227. One source claims that Leete's poster was on display 'everywhere' by January 1915, but also says it was accompanied by PRC 133, 'Forward to Victory', which was not issued until September 1915: M MacDonagh, *In London During the Great War: The Diary of a Journalist*, London, 1935, p 51.

6. PRO, WO 106/367, 'Parliamentary Recruiting Committee: Publications Sub-Department Report', c. May 1916, pp 7–8. A photograph of the PRC office in December 1915, with PRC 113 over the entrance, is in BL, Add. Mss. 54,192. For the top 15 PRC posters in terms of numbers produced, see Appendix B.

7. The issue of cigarette cards is noted in *Billposter*, 1 August 1915, p 13.

8. 'The Power of the Poster', *Billposter*, 1 June 1915, p 115.

9. 'A Poster Gallery', *Manchester Guardian*, 29 March 1915, p 6; 'Recruiting by Poster', *Windsor Magazine*, June 1915, p 4; '2,500,000 Posters', *Daily Chronicle*, 24 June 1915, p 3; PRO WO 106/367, 'Parliamentary Recruiting Committee: Publications Sub-Department Report', c. May 1916, pp 7–8.

10. *Hansard*, House of Commons, 10 June 1915, col 350 [L C Money]; 'The Editor's Chair', *Placard*, July 1915, p 3; *Billposter*, 1 August 1916, p 136. The publicity department of the Central London Recruiting Depot was run by a former advertising agent named F W Cooke: PRO WO 106/371, 'Visit to Chief London Recruiting Office', 17 May 1916, p 3.

11. N Hiley, 'Sir Hedley Le Bas and the Origins of Domestic Propaganda in Britain 1914–1917', *Journal of Advertising History*, Vol 10, No. 2, 1987, p 34.

12. H F Le Bas, 'Advertising for an Army' in H F Le Bas (ed), *The Lord Kitchener Memorial Book*, London, 1916, n p; E Field, *Advertising: The forgotten years*, London, 1958, p 29.

13. H Simonis, *The Street of Ink: An intimate history of journalism*, London, 1917, p 272; 'Alfred Chew Leete' *Times*, 19 June 1933, p 19; Darracott and Loftus, *First World War Posters*, p 37.

14. *Kinematograph Weekly*, 3 December 1914, supplement pp xxviii–xxix; *London Opinion*, 19 December 1914, p 387; P V Bradshaw, *Art in Advertising: A study of British and American pictorial publicity*, London, 1925, p 334; T Driberg, '*Swaff': The life and times of Hannen Swaffer*, London, 1974, pp 68–9; W A Campbell, 'James Crossley Eno', in D J Jeremy (ed), *Dictionary of Business Biography, Vol 2*, London, 1984, p 294.

15. H St G Ogden 'The Man Who Induced the Government to Advertise', *Higham's Magazine*, April 1916, pp 14–15; T W Smith, *Spilt Ink*, London, 1932, pp 115–7.

16. Le Bas, 'Advertising for an Army', n p; H F Le Bas, 'How Advertising Helped to Win the War', *Ways and Means*, 26 April 1919, p 245; Le Bas papers, scrapbook of 'Press Cuttings, Telegrams, Letters, etc', p 187, cutting from *Daily Telegraph*, 3 February 1916. I am grateful to Mrs Mary Abrahams for access to Sir Hedley Le Bas's surviving papers.

17. T Russell, *Commercial Advertising*, London, 1920, p 124; Le Bas papers, cutting from *Star*, 20 February 1920.

18. A copy of Partridge's cartoon, which does not bear a PRC imprint, is in the Le Bas papers.

19. Imperial War Museum, Department of Art, P A Gunn to B Kitts, 3 December 1971, pp 1–2, with enclosure 'Extract from Memoirs of Arthur L Gunn'.

20. '2,500,000 posters', *Daily Chronicle*, 24 June 1915, p 3; 'The Parliamentary Committee', *Times Recruiting Supplement*, 3 November 1915, p 4; PRO, WO 106/367, 'Parliamentary Recruiting Committee: Publications Sub-Department Report', c. May 1916, p 4; BL, Add. Mss. 59, 192, R H Davies to British Museum, 4 May 1967, ff. 3–4; M Rickards, *Posters of the First World War*, London, 1968, p 12.

21. 'British Posters in USA', *Selling and Advertising*, August 1917, p 263.

22. 'A Personal Word to the Chief Party Whips', *Daily Mail*, 25 March 1912; 'Political Propaganda and the Advertising Expert', *Advertising World*, April 1912, pp 387–9; C F Higham, *Scientific Distribution*, London, 1916, pp 145–6.

23. G B Pusey, 'Advertising the Territorial Force', *Printer's Ink*, October 1913, p 6; 'Why Not Advertise the Army?', *Daily Mail*, 13 November 1913, p 6; W A C Denny, 'Advertising the Army', *Advertising World*, December 1913, pp 845–6; C C Freer, *The Inner Side of Advertising: A practical handbook*, London, 1924, p 298.

24. 'Notes of the Week', *New Age*, 3 September 1914; 'Origin of Posters', *Placard*, October 1915, p 22.

25. 'An Army Raised by Advertising', *Daily Mail*, 5 March 1915, p 4; 'Secrecy', *Daily Mail*, 19 April 1915, p 4. The Pianola advertisement was specifically praised in a book published by Le Bas: J M Allison, 'Press Advertising', in W S M Knight (ed), *The Business Encyclopaedia and Legal Adviser*, London, 1907, Vol VII, p 243.

26. 'What to Do With Our War Posters', *Bystander*, 8 September 1915, p 345; *Selling and Advertising*, November 1915, p 91 and January 1916, supplement p ii, 'British Posters in USA', August 1917, p 263; Avery, 'National Advertising in Posters', pp 110–111.

27. *Billposter*, 1 August 1915, p 10; 'The Formation of a Coalition Government', *Times History of the War*, Vol 5, Part 60, 12 October 1915, p 295; 'A Review of Recruiting', *English Review*, December 1915, p 503; 'The Recruiting Crisis', *Quarterly Review*, April 1916, p 571.

28. F S Oliver, *Ordeal by Battle*, London, 1915, p 369; 'An Enquiry into Vulgarity', *New Statesman*, 4 September 1915, p 511.

29. 'Notes of the Week', *New Age*, 3 September 1914, p 411; ' From a Recruiting Office Note Book'; *Journal of the Royal United Service Institution*, November 1916, p 831.

30. Oliver, *Ordeal by Battle*, pp 370–1; 'Recruiting by Poster', *Windsor Magazine*, June 1915, p 3; BL, Add. Mss. 59, 192, PRC 'Minute Book No. 1', GPC meeting of 26 August 1915, f. 33; PRO WO 106/367, 'Parliamentary Recruiting Committee: Publications Sub-Department Report', c. May 1916, p 9; A Marwick, *The Deluge: British Society and the First World War*, London, 1965, p 52.

31. PRO, WO 106/364, notes from an interview with Colonel Gossett, 22 May 1916, p 4; WO 106/367, 'Parliamentary Recruiting Committee: Publications Sub-Department Report', c. May 1916, p 2; Sessional Papers 1921, 'General Annual Reports on the British Army . . . 1 October 1913 to 30 September 1919', HMSO, London, 1921, p 60.

32. 'The Householder's Circular', *Times*, 6 January 1915, p 4; 'Distribution of Posters', *Times*, 30 March 1915, p 5; 'A Poster Gallery', *Manchester Guardian*, 29 March 1915, p 6; 'Recruiting by Poster', *Windsor Magazine*, June 1915, p 6; '2,500,000 Posters', *Daily Chronicle*, 24 June 1915, p 3.

33. Cambridge University Library, WRP Posters collection, PRC circular dated 25 March 1915; 'Distribution of

Posters', *Times*, 30 March 1915, p 5; Sessional Papers 1914–16, 'Report from the Select Committee on Publications and Debates Reports' (1915), p 3 [evidence of F Atterbury, 20 April 1915]; 'Recruiting by Poster', *Windsor Magazine*, June 1915, p 16; PRO WO 106/367, 'Parliamentary Recruiting Committee: Publications Sub-Department Report', c. May 1916, p 6.

34. C F G Masterman, 'Why the Workman Enlists', *Nation*, 11 September 1915, p 763; H W Wilson and J A Hammerton (eds) *The Great War : Volume 5*, Amalgamated Press, London, 1916, p 397; PRO WO 106/367, 'Parliamentary Recruiting Committee: Publications Sub-Department Report', c. May 1916, p 2.

35. BL, Add. Mss., 59, 192, 'Minutes Book No. II', meeting of 11 October 1915, f. 3; PRO WO 106/367, 'Parliamentary Recruiting Committee: Publications Sub-Department Report', c. May 1916, p 2.

36. 'Origin of Army Posters', *Placard*, October 1915, p 24; 'On the Hoardings', *Advertising World*, November 1915, p 466.

37. J Brophy, 'Chants and Sayings' in J Brophy and E Partridge, *Songs and Slang of the British Soldier: 1914–1918*, 3rd edition, London, 1931, p 194; E Partridge, *A Dictionary of Catchphrases*, London, 1977, p 133.

38. 'Tall Tales', *Minden Magazine*, March 1916, p 13; Brophy, 'Chants and Sayings', pp 194, 270–1; Partridge, *Dictionary of Catchphrases*, p 241; K Adrian and A Badrock, *Edison Bell Winner Records*, E Bayly, 2nd edition 1989, Winner 2974.

39. Catalogue of War Literature, pp 2–19; Darracott and Loftus, *First World War Posters*, p 63.

40. PRO WO 106/367, 'Report by PRC Publications and Publicity Sub-Departments', 1916, pp 7–8.

41. Many different collections of posters were examined, the most important being those of the Imperial War Museum (Art Department Poster Collection), British Library (Tab. 11748a), and Cambridge University Library (WRP collection). Further information comes from the Stationery Office *Catalogue of War Literature Issued by HM Government, 1914–1919*, HMSO, London, 1921, and from the article 'Recruiting by Poster' in the *Windsor Magazine* of June 1915.

Allied prisoner of war attitudes to the fall of Singapore and the 'Selerang Barrack Square Incident'

R P W Havers

Rob Havers is a PhD student at Pembroke College, Cambridge.

At Singapore, in February 1942, the British Army suffered an ignominious defeat. The 'greatest disaster in the history of British arms'[1] was compounded by the psychological impact of the nature of that defeat and the recognized underperformance of the troops involved in the campaign. The Japanese, too, were well aware of the nature of their victory and the mass surrender of so many Allied soldiers only added to their success. In stark contrast surrender for the average Japanese soldier, at this early juncture of the war, was abhorrent. For many thousands of Allied soldiers the Malayan 'campaign' amounted to little more than a disastrous military action and an abrupt surrender, followed by the peculiar, unrestricted existence that characterised the early months at the Changi prison camp.[2] Only eight months later however, many of those same men were risking their lives against far greater odds than they had experienced in the fighting for Singapore and Malaya. What became known as 'the Selerang Barrack Square Incident' occurred as a direct result of the POWs at Changi refusing to sign a form demanding that they refrain from attempting to escape, a feat that was universally acknowledged to be all but impossible given the geographical location of Singapore and the distribution of Japanese forces in the region. The Japanese authorities, faced with a unanimous refusal, incarcerated the POWs within the confines of the Selerang barrack square until such a time as their demands were met. Although the POWs eventually capitulated, they did so only after the Japanese issued a formal military order instructing them to do so, thus removing the voluntary element of the pledge that was so objectionable to the prisoners. Why then did these men resist the Japanese demand to sign the parole forms? Why did these soldiers choose to stand upon a point of honour and endure cramped and insanitary conditions rather than sign a simple paper pledge?

The significance of the events at Selerang between 30 August and 5 September however, lie not in the refusal to sign the Japanese forms *per se,* nor in the fact that the POWs themselves believed they had won a moral victory, but rather in the light that this action sheds on contemporary POW attitudes to the Japanese, to their fellow prisoners and, most interestingly of all, toward the humiliating defeat at Singapore itself. This article is intended to demonstrate that the impact of the collapse of Singapore was a constant preoccupation for the Allied soldiers who had survived it, at least until 5 September 1942. It will show that the extent to which the Allied POWs were actually resisting the signing of a paper pledge was negligible. In fact these men were actually seeking to re-establish their credentials as soldiers and believed that the dispute over the forms was an ideal medium through which to achieve this. The 'Selerang Incident' although of only a few days' duration stands as the high point of POW resistance to a brutal and uncompromising enemy. Although the POWs failed to oblige the Japanese to remove their demands, their real achievement should be judged by what their resistance actually amounted to, rather than what it failed to secure.

The 'Selerang Incident', although mentioned frequently in the literature concerned with Changi, is generally under-emphasised in terms of the way the POWs themselves perceived the resistance to the Japanese demands. Similarly, it is invariably discussed in isolation from the events prior to August 1942 and as though it had no significant ramifications for those involved. This article draws on contemporary diaries and journals, seeks to place the 'Selerang Incident' more firmly within the context of the fall of Singapore and aims to provide a new perspective on the reasons that underpinned the POW resistance, on the fall of Singapore and the nature of the defeat there, as well as discussing the initial conditions that prevailed at Changi.

The Loss of Malaya and the Fall of Singapore.

Singapore, mighty fortress,
Guardian of the East.
The Japanese didn't think so,
They took it in a week.[3]

The Japanese attacked Malaya on 8 December 1941, simultaneously launching attacks on Pearl Harbor, Thailand and Hong Kong.[4] Despite initial RAF air sorties of modest success, the Japanese established themselves ashore at Singora and Patani in Thailand and at Kota Bharu in northern Malaya.[5] The consistent retreat that characterised the ensuing British strategy in Malaya was designed to ensure that British forces were not destroyed but instead retained their essential integrity as fighting units so that they might still form part of the long-range defence of Singapore itself.[6] The initial British plan, Operation 'Matador', was to advance into neutral Thailand in order to forestall the Japanese advance by securing the narrow Isthmus of Kra. This brave tactical initiative required twenty-four hours notice, *before* any Japanese landing, to ensure maximum success. Political fears over the violation of Thai neutrality and the subsequent detrimental impact on American opinion, resulted in indecision until the Japanese invasion force was off the Thai coast. By the time the true aim of this force was apparent, and it was realised that it was not a bluff designed to prompt a British violation of Thai neutrality, the critical moment had passed. Lieutenant-General A E Percival, GOC Malaya, was faced with either committing his 11th Indian Division to meet the invaders from Singora, in unfavourable country, or staying put.[7] He decided to face the Japanese from the prepared positions already occupied by the Indian Division and thus 'Matador' was never executed.[8] The ancillary plan, the advance by the 'Krohcol' force on the small town of Kroh in Thailand to hold the strategically vital position known as the 'ledge', overlooking the main road from Patani into northern Malaya, was delayed by determined Thai resistance and here too the British failed to capitalise on what was sound strategic planning. The failure of British air power to prevent the landing of Japanese troops and the heavy losses inflicted by Japanese air attacks on RAF airfields, resulted in the decision to conserve the remainder for the defence of the naval base on Singapore island and the arrival of relief convoys. This decision effectively removed any air support from the army fighting in Malaya itself.[9]

By 12 December the Allied forces had begun a fighting withdrawal through Malaya. Despite some successful counter-attacks and ambushes, notably by the Australian Imperial Force at Gemas, the Allied formations were outfought and outmanoeuvred by experienced Japanese troops. The Japanese were generally operating without the handicap of a heavy load of personal equipment, unlike their opponents, and moving in groups small enough to infiltrate behind the prepared Allied positions. They also had complete air superiority and used this to full advantage, harrassing the retreating Allied columns. Lord Strabolgi, writing in 1942, considered that 'British soldiers . . . who had not long been in the country, could not identify an apparently harmless Malay farmer or fisherman who in reality was a disguised Japanese trooper'.[10] The Japanese also made extensive use of bicycles and employed tanks. The British forces, by way of contrast, had no tanks at all in the whole of the Malayan peninsula in the misguided belief that the terrain was unsuitable.[11]

Kuala Lumpur fell to the Japanese on 12 January 1942, along with extensive supplies that the retreating British forces had failed to destroy. By the end of January 1942 the British forces had retreated across the Johore causeway that linked Singapore to the mainland. The siege of Singapore had begun. On 30 January the remainder of the RAF, save for one squadron, were evacuated to the Dutch East Indies.[12] On 31 January at 08.15 the causeway was severed by a demolition charge. Despite various exhortations by the British Prime Minister,

Winston Churchill and General Wavell, the Supreme Allied Commander in the South-West Pacific, the siege of the island lasted only two weeks. Indeed, Churchill wrote of his surprise when the true state of the Singapore defences became apparent. He said:

> The possibility of Singapore having no landward defence no more entered my mind than that of a battleship being launched without a bottom.[13]

On 7 February the Japanese crossed the Johore straits and landed on the north-west side of Singapore island. Despite some post-war controversy over where exactly Percival had believed the attack would come from, the extent of his anticipaiion may be seen in the placing of the fresh British 18th Division in the north-east.[14] On 15 February, after the loss of the last major reservoir, General Percival surrendered unconditionally to the Japanese. His action was ostensibly to save the lives of the innumerable civilians sheltering on the island who had escaped from the north. The Japanese, however, were dangerously low on ammunition specifically and supplies in general and at one point believed that the British request for negotiations was aimed at securing a Japanese surrender.[15] Singapore, Britain's 'impregnable fortress' in the Far East had fallen in a most inglorious manner.[16] At 20.10 British forces officially ceased fire and the Malayan campaign was over.

Surrender and captivity

> *We were dumbfounded . . . For one mad second I thought the Japs must have had enough and were evacuating the island . . . I couldn't understand why we had to surrender.*[17]

The manner of the campaign and subsequent surrender have been extensively scrutinized and blame apportioned widely. The alleged 'guilt' for the failures in the campaign has been heaped on the pre-war planners and politicians responsible for defence policy in Malaya; the inadequate leadership of the British commanders in the field, particularly General Percival; the indiscipline of the Australians and the inexperience and poor quality of the Indian Army units. Irrespective of where the blame for the loss of Malaya and Singapore really lies, however, there is a single fact that every commentator can agree upon; the conduct of the war in Malaya and Singapore was mishandled and led to an unprecedented national and Imperial humiliation. This perception of the war in Malaya as a disaster, despite many brave actions by many men, is what underpins much of the subsequent commentary on events and characterises the manner in which the campaign is still remembered today. What is significant is that this perception was widely appreciated, at the time, by those who participated in the campaign.[18]

Ironically, much of the shock at the loss of Singapore was predicated upon the success of pre-war propaganda depicting the island as an 'impregnable fortress', the linchpin in the defence of Britain's Far East

Makeshift shelters constructed by cooks alongside a water truck are in the foreground of this view of Selerang square during the 'Incident', and in the background troops queue at the Regimental Aid Post. AWM Neg. No. 106530

Empire. This idea of Singapore was fostered partly because of the political reassurance that it provided to successive Australian Governments and also because £60m of taxpayer's money had been spent on the enormous naval complex. Popular perceptions of the island as a fortress served to convey the idea that this huge sum had been wisely spent and that value for money had been obtained.[19] The cruel realisation of defeat was thus exaggerated by the extent to which the fortress notion had been believed. Unlike the withdrawal of the BEF from France in June 1940, or of the Gallipoli expedition forces, an important image for the Australians, there was no heroic evacuation of the Malayan Army, neither was there a resolute 'fighting stand' as at Stalingrad or Corregidor, two contemporary examples of determined resistance demonstrated by Britain's principal allies, the USSR and USA respectively. Instead, the 'fortress' of Singapore had surrendered after a siege of just two weeks which followed seven weeks of continuous retreat. The Japanese undertook their invasion with inferior numbers in comparison to their British adversaries, although the extent to which this was appreciated at the time is unclear. What was clear at the time, however, was that the popular stereotype of the average Japanese soldier was racist and underestimated his martial qualities. The Japanese were alleged to be uniformly short, buck-toothed and myopic. This misguided belief, in turn, backfired. Widespread adherence to this description served only to sharpen the recriminations levelled against the forces charged with defending Malaya. Only after the Malayan campaign did this stereotype change and then, in a complete *volte-face,* the Japanese were portrayed equally unrealistically as supermen, capable of marching many miles and then fighting a battle, whilst subsisting on the bounty of the jungle or only 'a handful of rice a day'. This stereotype was only dispelled after fighting in New Guinea and Burma.[20] The weight of popular feeling concerned with the misconduct of the war in Malaya led Churchill to comment in a Secret Session of the House of Commons on 23 April 1942. He said:

> I do not wonder that requests should be made for an inquiry by a Royal Commission, not only into what took place upon the spot in the agony of Singapore but into all the arrangements which had been made beforehand. I am convinced, however, that this would not be good for our country, and that it would hamper the prosecution of the war. Australian accounts reflect upon the Indian troops. Other credible witnesses disparage the Australians . . . there is an endless field for recrimination.[21]

Churchill subsequently considered that an enquiry would be a positive action but should wait until after the cessation of hostilities. Despite the obvious opportunity afforded by his post-war premiership, the enquiry never materialised.

When the dispirited ground forces of Malaya Command eventually reached the island of Singapore, they were shocked to find that the principal reason for their sacrifices in Malaya itself, the extensive naval base, was already being destroyed in order to deny it to the Japanese. Lionel Wigmore, the official Australian War Historian wrote that:

> one of the greatest shocks suffered by the forces upon their withdrawal to the island was the discovery that it had been abandoned by the Navy and [the naval base] was being demolished. To many, including some senior officers, it seemed that the primary purpose of being in Malaya had disappeared . . .[22]

The detrimental impact upon morale was felt at all levels. Lieutenant-General Sir Henry Pownall was Chief of Staff to General Wavell.[23] On 5 February Pownall wrote in his diary that:

> Percival has decided, no doubt rightly, that he must withdraw to the Island in the next day or two. That is bad news. It means that the naval base has gone for good and the only reason for fighting for Singapore is to keep the base open . . . merely as an island Singapore is no more important than many another of the thousand islands round here.[24]

If Pownall felt this way, writing from the relative safety of Java, then the effect on the men involved in the actual fighting was probably far greater. The campaign had effectively been a continuous retreat, allowing for little rest on the part of the troops involved. By the time these units reached Singapore they were dispirited and exhausted. The pre-emptive destruction of the naval base only lowered morale still further. The overwhelming question now was whether a resolute stand should be made on Singapore itself. This course of action was essentially a futile one as without the prize of the naval facilities the island itself was worthless. In addition, the utility of the base could not have been maintained once the Malayan province of Johore had been abandoned. The naval base was located on the north shore of Singapore island and thus within range of enemy artillery firing across the narrow Johore strait. The whole notion of the 'Singapore Fortress' may be seen to be fundamentally flawed. Even had the island been adequately fortified the fact that the base's vulnerable location relied on the maintenance of Allied control of large areas of Malaya only serves to illustrate further the ambiguous and politically motivated aims that drove defence policy in the Far East. Despite these inherent contradictions, however, a determined last stand was deemed the best solution by many, not the least being Prime Minister Churchill himself. On 19 January Winston Churchill had declared that 'no question of surrender should be entertained until after protracted fighting among the ruins of Singapore City'.[25] Later, Churchill urged the defenders of Singapore to 'fight to the death' with the 'honour of the British Empire and of the British Army at stake'.[26] On the same day General Wavell issued a similar exhortation; he declared that 'our whole fighting reputation is at stake . . . it will be disgraceful if we yield our boasted fortress of Singapore'.[27] The absence of any practical gain to be made from further resistance is apparent. Instead there is an identifiable need for some form of atonement for the failures in the campaign as a whole in the high command communications of this period. Percival himself addressed the problems of desertion and unauthorised withdrawals that had bedevilled the whole campaign. He stated in a communique that:

> . . . the troops have not shown the fighting spirit which is expected of men in the British Empire. It will be a lasting disgrace to us if we are to be defeated by an army of gangsters our inferior numbers in strength.[28]

Reinforcements continued to arrive in Singapore up until the surrender. On 22 January the 44th Indian Infantry Brigade arrived; composed of very young and partially trained recruits, it was held back for 'further training'. On 24 January additional Australian troops of the 2/4th Machine Gun Battalion landed. The British 18th Division was ordered to Singapore whilst *en route* to India and arrived on 29 January. This force had only two weeks before the surrender and no time to contribute effectively to the defence.[29] The sense of futility and impotence experienced by these men in particular must have been enormous. Sir Richard Sharp, in February 1942 a subaltern with the Royal Northumberland Fusiliers, wrote:

> So this is what we had come for. This was the end of our two years of training, of 13 weeks on board ship, to spend a few days in miserable fighting and give in.[30]

The strategic ineptitude, or otherwise, that contributed to the fall of Singapore is not the principal subject of this article. However, it will be seen that these practical and perceived inadequacies impacted quite strongly upon the psychological response of many POWs toward the Japanese, not so far as defeat itself was the obvious reason for their imprisonment, but rather that the manner of such a defeat had served to remove from the minds of many men the reassurance that they had 'done their regiment proud' before 'going into the bag'. The absence of this feeling led in large measure to their determination to resist the Japanese demands to sign the parole forms in August–September 1942. Although the impact of the surrender and the manner of the defeat are hard either to gauge or to quantify accurately, the frequent references to the nature of the surrender amongst the many diaries and memoirs of POWs captured at Singapore would indicate that it was of acute concern for the early part of their captivity and an on-going source of discomfiture to a great many men.

By 1941 the Changi 'Fortress', as the Japanese had ironically termed it, was complete. In a little over fifteen years a large area of virgin jungle at the easternmost tip of Singapore island had been cleared and transformed into 'one of the most modern and best equipped military bases anywhere in the world'.[31] On 16 February 1942, the day after the official surrender of Allied troops on Singapore, approximately 35,000 British and 15,000 Australians were obliged by their Japanese captors to march from defensive positions scattered around the island and to converge upon Changi.[32] The Changi camp had no wall or fence round it until the prisoners themselves were ordered to begin the construction of confining perimeters.[33] Basil Peacock, a British Officer wounded in the last days of fighting for Singapore, wrote in his account of his life as a POW that 'we had put up the barbed wire, and to a certain extent were providing our own guards, which I thought a bit queer'.[34] Few Japanese entered the area, a practice that would continue until the Camp moved to Changi Gaol in May 1944. This fact helped to reinforce the air of unreality which existed for the many POWs, one of neither captivity nor of complete freedom despite the fact that they moved freely around Singapore town in the first few months after February. This was, in effect, a very peculiar prison camp, one without visible signs of confinement nor of a recognisable routine enforced by the Japanese authorities.[35] It was a place in which, 'except for a few forbidden areas, we were left entirely to our own devices'.[36] Lieutenant Colonel D S Ainger was prompted to remark in his journal at the time that, 'we seldom saw any Japanese and it was a peaceful existence, but oh! so boring'.[37] Two days after the surrender of Singapore, the Japanese imposed a 'colour bar', segregating all Indian ranks from their British and Australian comrades and placing them in a special camp at Farrar Park.[38] These soldiers composed the balance of the Allied troops captured in the surrender. This segregation was aimed at facilitating the efforts of the Japanese to persuade Indians and other nationalities that their future lay in an active participation with the 'Greater East Asia Co-prosperity Sphere' that the Japanese planned for South East Asia, rather than with their former colonial masters. This act of segregation ensured that the men in the barrack square were overwhelmingly British and Australian with a number of Dutchmen also in evidence.

The Selerang Barrack Square Incident

I cannot describe the feeling of claustrophobia which prevailed and shudder even now when I think of those horrible few days.[39]

By the end of August the number of prisoners confined within the Changi area had diminished considerably. Work parties were dispersed to sites around Singapore Island and other groups had gone to Burma and Borneo.[40] On 16 August 1942 the Japanese had removed all 'officers of the rank of Colonel and upwards' from Changi; this group included General Percival.[41] In anticipation of this move Percival appointed Lieutenant Colonel E B Holmes of the Manchester Regiment as Commander British and Australian POWs and Major-General Callaghan appointed Lieutenant Colonel F G Galleghan, 2/30th Bn. AIF as Commander of the AIF.[42]

On 19 August 1942 a new Japanese officer, Major-General Shipei Fukuye, was appointed GOC POW camps in Malaya, replacing Colonel Sugita.[43] The arrival of Fukuye precipitated what would become known as the 'Selerang Barrack Square Incident'. After six months of captivity the POW body at Changi was not particularly robust. Holmes wrote that 'officers and men were still dazed by the events of Feb.'.[44] The:

> health of troops gave cause for anxiety. Deaths during this month [August] totalled 45, mostly dysentery. Diphtheria was increasing alarmingly and dysentery was still rampant and represented 35% of the cases in hospital. In addition, beriberi was increasing and accounted for 10% of the cases in hospital and skin diseases were very prevalent.[45]

On 30 August the senior Allied officers were presented with a demand that all POWs sign a 'non-escape declaration' form.[46] The wording on the Japanese parole form stated that:

> I, the undersigned, hereby solemnly swear on my honour that I will not, under any circumstances, attempt escape.[47]

The next day, 31 August, at an Area Commander's Conference:

> it was unanimously decided not to sign. At the insistence of the Japanese the whole matter was freely put to the camp and finally only four other ranks wished to, and were allowed to sign. Their parole forms were sent to the Imperial Japanese Army next day.[48]

The Japanese informed Holmes that those not signing the parole would be subject to unspecified 'measures of severity'.[49] On 1 September the Japanese instructed Holmes that 'all those not willing to sign would be prepared to move to Salarang [*sic*] Square by 1830 hours next day, 2 Sep. '42'.[50] Also at this time Holmes submitted an amendment to the wording of the Japanese form, adding the clause 'without incurring the death penalty'. This revision was rejected by the Japanese.[51] At 0130 hrs on 2 September instructions to move were provisionally issued and accommodation allotted.[52] While no move to Selerang Barracks was to be made prior to the receipt of Japanese orders to that effect, the AIF commenced the necessary work of digging latrine pits on the square itself. At 1330 hrs the Japanese gave the order to move.[53]

That day Lieutenant Colonel C Wilkinson wrote in his diary, 'given orders to march out to a concentration camp'.[54] Lieutenant J A Richardson said that 'I have never seen quite so hectic a mass trek, 17,000 on foot with all manner of trucks (engineless) and carts.'[55] Captain Alan Rodgers, AIF, watched the influx of men to Selerang:

> It was a sight never to be forgotten, to see the English come over, there seems a never ending stream of them, and they brought their possessions over by all manner of means—most of them were carried by hand, but there were all kinds of improvised vehicles. There were hand carts of the most varied description, the greatest part of them obviously very home made. They ran a gamut [*sic*] from one wheel to four and maybe even more, for all I know. There were all sorts of animals brought

> over—a herd of goats, about eight in all, several crates of chickens and ducklings, three monkeys, and half a dozen dogs, they poured over in what seemed to us a never ending stream and many of them were in the last stages of exhaustion, because the majority of them were undertaking a journey of three miles or so, in the blazing sun of the hottest part of the afternoon . . .[56]

The conditions in the barrack square at Selerang were cramped in the extreme.[57] Major A N Thompson, AIF camp quartermaster, estimated that the total confined was 14,609 and that the strength of the AIF alone was 1,897.[58] This enlarged total occupied an area that had been originally designed to accommodate a single battalion in peacetime, around 600–700 men. Lieutenant Baillies, one of the men fortunate enough to be accommodated inside, recorded in his diary that 'we have the ground floor of one (barrack) block, there are 800 of us in it, and each man has exactly 2ft by 5½ ft'.[59] Captain Inglefield made the understated observation that 'those who had to sleep outside were not on a good wicket'.[60] The Japanese demand for signatures appeared firm.

On 2 September Holmes and Galleghan, together with their senior officers, were obliged to watch the execution of four men who had been caught trying to escape. The execution would have a strong bearing on the course of events. They were Corporal Breavington and Private Gale, AIF, Private Waters, The East Surrey Regiment, and Private Fletcher, Royal Army Ordnance Corps.[61] Holmes 'protested vehemently' at this action and submitted a plea asking for clemency.[62] This was refused and the four men were shot by Indian troops on the beach at Changi. This exercise was rendered the more distasteful by the fact that the four men had made their escape attempts several months earlier. Major Francis Magee wrote:

> I knew that these four men had made previous individual attempts to escape, the Japanese punishment for which was death, and that the Imperial Japanese Army had returned them after capture to our camp to be held by us for punishment. They were NOT in close custody. I knew that Pte WATERS . . . had attempted to escape from a camp in Singapore as far back as May and been apprehended by the Japanese almost immediately. Since then he had been taken on our strength and to all intents and purposes, was an ordinary prisoner of war, subject to NO special restrictions.[63]

Similarly the two AIF men, Corporal Breavington, an Englishman born in Southend in Essex, and Private Gale had also escaped in May. They had rowed a small boat for 200 miles to the island of Colomba where they were arrested and taken to the military hospital on the island of Davao. They were returned to Singapore on 1 July 1942, with Breavington going to hospital and Gale to Curran Camp.[64] At the execution site Breavington pleaded for the life of his friend, Private Gale, claiming that he had ordered the younger man to accompany him. This action, together with his general demeanour throughout the ordeal, prompted Galleghan to write that Breavington 'was the bravest man I have ever seen' in a subsequent letter to Breavington's wife.[65] Instead of undermining the POWs' resolve the executions in fact had the opposite effect, that of hardening the British and Australian determination to resist. News of the shooting was widespread in Changi within hours of the event. Lieutenant Baillies mentions the executions in his diary, recording that 'they were shot by the Sikhs and I'm told it was clumsily done'.[66]

The perimeter of the barrack square was surrounded by armed guards, many of them men from the British-Indian Army who had been persuaded or cajoled to join the Japanese.[67] E Holden remembers that, 'if anyone overstepped the boundary line, he was stabbed at with bayonets by the guard of Sikhs who constantly patrolled the roadway'.[68] Lieutenant Baillies wrote, 'There have been several small incidents, prisoners being beaten up by Sikh guards for putting a foot inadvertently over the boundary line'.[69] The Japanese also mounted machine guns around the square and increased the number of Sikh and Japanese guards patrolling the perimeter.[70] To make conditions as unbearable as possible the Japanese cut off the mains water supply to the barrack buildings. Drinking water was now only available from two stand-pipe taps established in the square itself.[71] Consequently, the water ration was reduced to only one pint, per man, per day. This meagre quantity had to suffice for cooking, washing and drinking.[72] To compound matters the barrack square afforded no shelter for the majority of men exposed to the harsh tropical sun. J W Franks remembered:

> the heat was unbearable. We had no cover and were exposed to the sun all day. We were crammed in like sardines surrounded by barbed wire. It was impossible to lie down, we squatted in the sun with our sweating comrades.[73]

In addition, the severing of the main water supply obviously rendered all the lavatories in the barracks themselves unusable. Sanitation was thus an immediate and pressing concern and orders were issued that sanitation work was to have priority over all other activities.[74] To overcome this problem, bore-holes, up to forty feet deep, were sunk into the parade-ground. This necessitated large gangs of POWs cutting through the thick bitumen of the parade ground surface. The digging of these improvised toilet facilities went on around the clock. C Coombs, a Signaller with the 9th Division Signals, wrote on 2 September that he had laboured for two hours on 'bore-hole' detail that day; from 8.30 pm to 9.30 pm in the evening and also from 3.30 am until 4.30 am. The early morning detail at least had the advantage of avoiding the intense heat.[75] Despite the immense effort devoted to latrine digging Colonel Wilkinson remarked two days later that 'the queue for the urinals is 200 yards long almost every day'.[76] The Japanese had reluctantly provided a supply of wood from which carpenters manufactured covers for the toilets dug into the square. This helped to stem the danger of disease spread by flies. On 3 September Lieutenant Colonel Wilkinson wrote in his diary that, 'we obviously can't last long under these conditions'.[77] On the same day the Japanese announced that the demand for signatures was the result of a policy formulated in Tokyo and there could be no compromise.[78]

Signaller Coombs commented on the significance of the impact of the 'Tokyo' aspect of the order on the prisoners, many of whom noted this in their diaries. Coombs wrote on 3 September that 'The Japs stated that the forms had been issued from Tokyo and that they would go to any "measures of severity" to get them signed'.[79] Lieutenant Baillies confirms this position, commenting that 'the Japs say the order to sign the forms has come from Tokyo, and there can be no compromise'.[80]

In his diary entry for 4 September Lieutenant Colonel Wilkinson wrote 'Friday. We are still hoping the IJA[81] will amend their forms to allow us to sign with honour. But if not we will have to give in. Men in wonderful spirits'.[82]

The amendment hoped for by Wilkinson was a simple but significant one. He, along with the senior Allied officers, wished the Japanese formally to order the POWs to sign rather than have them do so, ostensibly, of their own volition, the coercion in the square notwithstanding. Simultaneously Sir Richard Sharp recorded the determination of the Japanese to press home their demands:

> on the third day, [4 September] they cut the water ration by half: and the doctors said the position was too serious to continue.[83]

At a Commander's conference the Deputy Director of Medical Services stated that 'today (4 September) was the latest day' on which the POWs could act without casualties.[84] That same day Lt. Baillies recorded that 'Our medical authorities estimate that diseases will be a serious consideration in three or four days, already the dysentery and diphtheria is spreading fast'.[85]

The Japanese sought to capitalise on the worsening conditions. An area of the barrack square had been set aside to serve as a makeshift hospital. When the main POW body had been obliged to move to Selerang the hospital had remained at Roberts Barracks. On 4 September General Fukuye threatened to move the hospital, together with all the patients, into the confines of the Selerang square as well. This threat was a serious and potentially a deadly one. S Warren, a bombardier with the 135th Field Regiment, Royal Artillery, wrote:

> the Japs (have) decided to move the hospital to Selerang. Problems. Any movement would kill all the seriously ill patients and battle casualties instantly. The highly infectious diseases would spread unchecked through the packed square.[86]

The cramped conditions and the inefficient sanitary provisions meant that any new infusion of contagious diseases from the hospitalised men would prove highly dangerous, to say nothing of the potentially disastrous effect of movement upon the battle casualties. Lieutenant Baillies wrote:

> Unless we sign, the hospital will also be moved into the area besides us. This involves another 7,000 men in all conditions of sickness, many of whom the move would kill.[87]

The threat to move Roberts Hospital was a significant one and Holmes later commented that 'this largely influenced the final decision to sign the parole form in order to save life'.[88]

With the position worsening Holmes continued to negotiate. At the Area Commanders' Conference at 1245 hrs on 4 September it had been proposed 'that Formation Comds. were prepared to sign if a direct order was given by the IJA to the Comd. Brit. and Aust. Troops' and that the following draft order had been submitted, 'It is the order of the IJA that all officers, NCOs and men will sign the following: [then declaration as at present]'.[89] The Japanese, however, refused to incorporate the order to sign within the form. It 'was then represented that we would sign if we received a written order in the form of a separate letter'.[90] At 1600 hrs Galleghan attended a conference at Malaya Command where he was informed that Holmes had been ordered to the Japanese HQ and instructed to take with him Japanese Order No. 17, dated 2 September, which instructed the concentration of all POWs in Selerang barrack square. In its place Holmes was handed a new order, although similarly dated and numbered, which *ordered* all personnel to sign the declaration.[91] The process of signing of the forms began immediately.

On 5 September, Lieutenant Baillies wrote that 'Colonel Holmes has asked us to sign on his responsibility, apparently the Japs compromised to the extent of admitting that this was under their orders, under stress, and not voluntary.'[92] Holmes had succeeded in persuading the Japanese to change their demand for signatures to a 'military order' to do so. This action fundamentally altered the perception of the stand-off for the POWs. Holmes wrote 'our current existence will result, in a very few days, in the outbreak of epidemic and . . . the inevitable death of many'.[93]

In retrospect, the Japanese decision seems strange as the POWs appeared on the verge of a capitulation without any Japanese compromise being apparent. However, for the Japanese the distinction between ordering and coercing the signatures may well have been a negligible one. The 'Selerang Barrack Square Incident' was over, the ramifications of the events that took place there, however, would last far longer.

The implications of the resistance to Japanese demands

Lieutenant W H Baillies made this entry in his diary on 30 August 1942, the day the Japanese made their demands known:

> The Japanese want us to sign a parole form giving our word not to attempt to escape. Nobody has agreed to do this and we are to parade at 9 am tomorrow morning. I am afraid this will be a bit unpleasant, the Japs don't seem to realise the unreasonableness of their request.[94]

Gilbert Inglefield considered at the time that the declaration was 'ridiculous and the crowning insult'.[95] The actual degree to which the Japanese believed these parole forms would prevent escape attempts must surely have been minimal. The POWs themselves believed that signatures obtained following a direct Japanese order absolved the individual from the moral responsibility of fulfilling the conditions. Equally, it is difficult to believe that, had any forms been signed as a direct result of the pressure applied in the barrack square, these would have had any greater moral hold over the actions of the individual who had been obliged to sign, after having experienced such conditions. If this is so then the POWs themselves, apparently keenly aware of such academic dilemmas, would have been equally absolved of any responsibility had they signed *before* the military order was issued but *after* being subjected to the privations in the square. Indeed Gilbert Inglefield asserted that 'ideologists maintained that a promise exacted by threats of violence was not morally binding'.[96] Thus being confined and bullied alone would seem to have satisfied these conditions. The POWs at Selerang endured these privations and held out until a military order was issued. General Percival, although at this point on Formosa, was himself asked, in

Colonel E B Holmes and Lieutenant Colonel F G Galleghan, 20 September 1945. AWM Neg. No. 117117

due course, to sign a similar declaration. His response, recorded in his memoirs of the Malayan campaign written in 1947, was one of consternation. He wrote, 'of course such a declaration was quite irregular' and that 'I have always thought that the Japanese only wanted it so that they could justify themselves in executing men who were caught trying to escape'.[97]

As Percival suggests, the forms were probably conceived as a way to justify severe punishment and to reap the benefits that the threat of such action would provide, in terms of the maintenance of Camp discipline.

> 'The extent to which the Japanese themselves would have considered the parole to be binding, had the situation been reversed, is perhaps significant in understanding their actions.'

However, it would seem that for the POWs themselves the issue had less to do with how 'binding' such a declaration was, nor under what conditions it would be so, and infinitely more to do with being seen to make a defiant stand of some kind. This would certainly explain why they resisted beyond the stage of being badly treated, even though they themselves had admitted that such treatment effectively invalidated any declarations obtained as a result. Instead, the POWs held on until the Japanese made a concession and were perceived as doing so. Stan Arneil believed that Holmes and Galleghan decided to use the *debacle* over the parole forms to demonstrate a point both to the Japanese and, more importantly, to their own men. Arneil wrote in his memoirs:

> It has been suggested that both Galleghan and Holmes used the incident to raise the morale of the troops and to demonstrate to them that even as prisoners they were still soldiers with contempt for the enemy.[98]

The response of the men to the refusal to sign was boisterous. Lieutenant C Thornton recorded the mood amongst the prisoners. He said:

> the men were determined to show these . . . Nips [author's blank inserted] that they couldn't play about with a British soldier's Honour, no matter how poor they were thought to be as fighting men.[99]

Thornton here refers to a pervading concern. The 'fighting spirit' of the British Army had not been shown in an overly favourable light at Singapore. Thornton was aware of this fact and deliberately addressed it in his diary. The immediate result of the Japanese action was to provide many POWs with an opportunity to demonstrate that their 'honour' actually was very much intact. Gilbert Inglefield comments that:

> Morale at no time in my POW experience was higher. A feeling of 'now we'll show 'em' came to each man after months of comparative ease.[100]

Gillies adds:

> It must be said that morale in general has been higher since this business started than for many a long day. There is no doubt that however it turns out, we have certainly secured a moral victory over the Nip in this matter.[101]

For the vanquished defenders of Singapore, in their own minds at least, their contribution to the war was far from over. Gilbert Inglefield wrote, 'It [was a] glorious opportunity and one that never occurred again. From now on we never really stood up to the Japs'.[102]

The situation at Selerang had residual benefits as well. Thornton makes a unique reference to the nature of Anglo-Australian relations before Selerang, saying that:

> The Japanese had been trying hard to ferment trouble between us and the Australians. If they had had any success it was lost entirely at Selerang. The Aussies 'mucked' in with us and we with them.[103]

Thornton, regrettably, supplies no evidence of how the Japanese were attempting to make trouble nor what may have persuaded them that either an existing, or a readily exploitable, rift between the British and the Australians would be fertile ground for sowing disharmony in the POW ranks. George Aspinall wrote:

> I don't know why and I don't mean to be hard on English people but they were appointed as the cooks. There was a small cookhouse at Selarang [*sic*] and we didn't think much of the way the pommy cooks treated the rice. Australians had become pretty good rice cooks by then, but the 'poms' created this gluey mess they called pap . . . but we got on pretty well with the British really.[104]

Scene in Selerang Square during the heavy rain, Singapore, September 1942. HU 32008

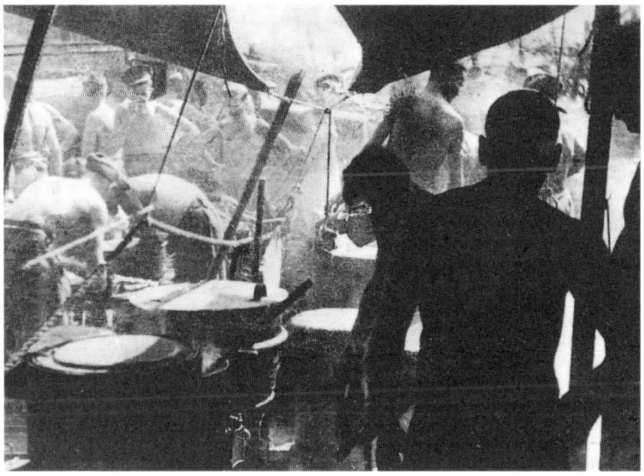

Selerang Square. Cutting up one of the goats in the British battalion cookhouse, September 1942. HU 32009

Two of the three 'lucky' ones who got a place on the verandah, Selerang Square, September 1942. HU 32012

A photograph of the Australian corner, showing men mending their socks. Selerang Square, Singapore, September 1942. HU 32015

Men sitting on their kit give a fair idea of the overcrowding at Selerang Square, September 1942. HU 32011

View of the latrines in the middle of Selerang Square, Singapore, September 1942. HU 32016

This opinion of English culinary skills is echoed by Sir Richard Sharp who commented that 'the English are conservative about their food and when you say rice to them, their automatic reaction is pudding'.[105]

This, however, appears to have been the practical extent of Anglo-Australian disharmony at Selerang. Indeed Padre Noel Duckworth was to write of the 'coming close together in friendship and mutual understanding between the men of the United Kingdom and the men of Australia'.[106] As far as general relations amongst the ranks were concerned Lieutenant Thornton considered 'the whole episode did more to cement the feeling of comradeship between officers and men than anything we ourselves could have devised'.[107]

On 2 September the Japanese had tried to persuade Holmes and Galleghan to order their men to sign by obliging them to attend the execution of four men, two Australians and two Britons, who had been found outside the Changi wire in May. Given the length of time between capture and punishment there had been a hope that the Japanese would be lenient. Instead, they took the opportunity to demonstrate their inflexiblility over escape and to press home their determination to see the parole forms signed.[108] The unspoken assumption of many Selerang diarists is that had Holmes and Galleghan been prepared to back down, then the lives of these four men might have been spared. As it was the event seems to have only strengthened the will to resist amongst the vast majority of POWs. This was due not only to reasons of anger at the deaths of four comrades. In the wake of the executions the *cordon-sanitaire* around the square was reinforced with additional, Japanese manned machine-guns. The increase in security around the square was born out of a concern that the executions might elicit a violent response. Major Gillies wrote that 'it is said that the Japs were firmly convinced that we were on the point of attempting a mass attack on them'.[109]

The Japanese precautions had quite the opposite effect to that which was intended. To the men in the square the effect of being regarded as a potential threat by the Japanese was a novel one for many. As a result it conferred a new sense of self-respect upon men long denied the acknowledgement that, although defeated, they were still in fact soldiers. These feelings found similar expression elsewhere. On 4 September, the day the decision to sign the forms was made, Lieutenant Colonel Wilkinson wrote in his diary that 'the NFs got a good chit for kit lay out and cleanliness of rooms—decision made to sign forms'.[110]

Although the POWs were on the verge of giving in to their captors' demands, the parallel demands of military discipline were making themselves felt as well. Wilkinson recorded the decision to sign almost as an aside, the decision apparently secondary to his obvious regimental pride at the 'chit' his unit had received. Thus, at the peak of the Japanese sanctions to enforce a surrender, military discipline is firm and pride in one's unit is still sufficiently strong and relevant to override other, more immediate considerations. For the thousands confined in the square at Selerang the act of resistance itself had, imperceptibly, become less a means to an end, than an end in itself.

The aftermath: POW reactions to the decision to sign.

'I hate the British. They are defeated, but there is no shame! You are stubborn, but have no pride. You endure, but have no courage. I hate the British!'[111]

On 30 August 1942, when the Japanese issued their demands, Colonel Galleghan had protested strongly that the troops should not be asked to make such a declaration on the reasonable grounds that such a promise implied a voluntary acquiescence to a Japanese proposal.[112] Following the Japanese decision on 4 September to issue a military order instructing the prisoners to sign, Colonel Holmes ordered the men at Changi to sign the Japanese forms.[113] George Aspinall remembers that Galleghan asked his men for their opinions about the decision and whether or not they should sign the declaration. He recalls Galleghan saying:

> Please discuss this amongst yourselves, and I will come back to you in half an hour to get your opinion. But my word to you is that we can sign this document and save further loss of life, because it would be signed under duress and not be binding.[114]

Whether this consultation period, mentioned only in accounts written by the men of the AIF, is indicative of a genuine egalitarianism amongst the Australian prisoners or merely an example of the astute Galleghan helping his men to overcome a difficult moral dilemma, is open to debate. Certainly Galleghan does not appear to have been anything less than a stern disciplinarian during his time at Changi. This apparently contemplative attitude is perhaps more indicative of the peculiarly delicate situation that had arisen during the tense stand-off between captors and captives and evidence to support the extent to which the declaration forms were, if not initially then ultimately, seen to be a crucial component in the bid to reconstruct morale, rather than as possessing an intrinsic value in their own right.

The decision to sign the declaration, even with the 'Japanese military order' caveat attached, was still a difficult one for many men at Selerang. Lieutenant Baillies remembered that 'Colonel Holmes ordered all of us to sign on his responsibility'.[115] E W Whincup, obviously concerned about the ramifications of affixing his name to such a document, wrote that 'fortunately, our CO provided each POW with a copy of the order, signed by him, to cover us should we eventually return to the United Kingdom'.[116]

Major Gillies commented:

> He [Colonel Holmes] insisted on getting a written order from the Japs to do so and also, I believe, got it in writing from them that they would in fact begin to shoot if he didn't give the order.[117]

This last sentence, concerning the alleged shooting threat, is not mentioned by any other diarist nor in any memoirs of Changi. C Coombs, however, mentions that he believed 'the Japs intended to cut off our water supply altogether (had we not signed within the next twenty-four hours)'.[118]

There was a genuine concern felt by the POWs about exactly how the signing of such a declaration, even under the direct orders of the Japanese and their own officers, would be viewed by the post-war British authorities. This is apparent by the fact that Holmes himself felt obliged to issue a supplementary letter addressing this matter.[119] Holmes assured his men that:

The final day. An officer signing the no escape form 'under duress' in Selerang Square. HU 32013

> It will naturally be my first endeavour to ensure on release that the position [regarding the signing of the 'no-escape' forms] is made clear to His Majesty's Government.[120]

Lieutenant Colonel Holmes's 'Special Order' to the men in the barrack square detailed the events leading up to the enforced move to Selerang, the negotiations that he and Galleghan had entered into on their behalf, as well as why they ultimately believed that signing the document under duress was acceptable.[121] This 'Order' is enlightening as it chronicles the events at Selerang from Holmes's own perspective but more importantly seeks to address the contemporary concerns of the men at Changi. Paragraph 9 reads as follows:

> I am fully convinced that His Majesty's Government only expects Prisoners of War not to give their parole when such parole is to be given voluntarily. This factor can in no circumstances be applicable to our present conditions. The responsibility for this decision rests with me, and with me alone and I fully accept it in ordering you to sign.[122]

The tone of Holmes's last line, concerning responsibility, perhaps indicates that he himself was not completely sure of his legal ground but was determined, at the least, that his men neither would nor should share any blame for their actions, undertaken as they were on his direct orders. Interestingly, Lieutenant R Garden, in his memoirs of being a prisoner of war at Pudu Gaol in Kuala Lumpur, wrote about his concerns and feelings when asked to sign a similar 'no-escape' declaration:

> They [here Garden is presumably referring to the senior Allied officers at Pudu] assured us that if we broke this parole agreement with the Japanese a plea that we signed under duress would exonerate us from fault in the eyes of British courts, though it would not of course prevent the Japanese from executing any of us caught after escaping.[123]

The Japanese, whilst being signatories to the Geneva Convention of 27 July 1929, had not ratified the document although they had agreed that it would be applied *mutatis mutandis.*[124] In 1943 prisoners held in Thailand presented their captors with a document detailing their circumstances in a bid to modify the extremes of treatment being meted out to them. Part two included a section on 'Suggestions' for the Japanese to take into consideration in the treatment of prisoners. This referred to the fall of Singapore, the nature of the capitulation there and the subsequent impact this was deemed to have had on the Japanese treatment of POWs. It read:

> It has been suggested [by the Japanese] that the unconditional surrender of Singapore placed the Prisoners outside the terms of the Hague convention. That is obviously not so. The position of any prisoner who is captured on the field of battle is that of unconditional surrender, but no one would suggest that he is not covered by the convention.[125]

The extent to which the collapse of Singapore influenced the subsequent treatment of POWs was an ever-present consideration for the men at Changi, as well as elsewhere. In this instance the men in Thailand who wrote this particular document considered that the Japanese had interpreted the nature of the surrender as putting them outside the bounds of international law and this convinced the POWs themselves that their mistreatment was being legally justified by the Japanese.[126] The POWs thus sought redress through a similarly legalistic framework. Although this document was written some time after the events at Selerang the dual ramifications are obvious and perhaps serve to demonstrate how signatures obtained following pressure in the barrack square or by the issuing of an order were considered equally acceptable to the Japanese military.

The decision to the sign the Japanese forms ended the 'Barrack Square Incident' and evoked some interesting and contradictory responses from the POWs. Lieutenant J A Richardson wrote simply that the incident was 'an interesting experiment which shows what the Japs will do'.[127] Lieutenant Colonel Wilkinson wrote 'the spirit of the men is wonderful'.[128] Lieutenant Baillies mentions that 'apparently the Japs compromised'.[129] In contrast to the general, almost congratulatory, tone of many diarists, however, is Captain J Ledingham, a surgeon with the 20th Combined General Hospital. Ledingham wrote bitterly of the whole Selerang experience in his diary. He was angry at the way in which he believed the senior officers had stage-managed the event to engineer what he saw only as a morale boosting activity. He wrote:

> We were informed that it [the no-escape declaration form] was a direct order. [This] satisfied our pseudo leaders and their pseudo honour.[130]

Ledingham's resentment at the recent activities is obvious. He continued:

> I am of the opinion that it was the wrong time for a defeated army to talk about honour. If more had been shown while defending Singapore I doubt I'd be a bloody prisoner of war now.[131]

Ledingham here cites the fall of Singapore, and the disappointing performances of the Allied troops defending it, as a specific reason for not entering into any game of brinkmanship with the Japanese, ironically, for broadly similar reasons as other diarists sought to justify that same resistance. Ledingham makes no mention of any positive psychological benefit having been derived from the time at Selerang. It is conceivable that Ledingham's role as a surgeon gave him a greater insight into the negative impact of such a demonstration upon the health of POWs already suffering from seven months of incarceration. The memoirs of E Holden, although not as uncompromisingly negative as Ledingham, raise similar doubts about the practical wisdom of resisting the Japanese demands. Holden declares that:

> Any thought of escape was out of the question. A glance at the map will show you that Singapore is in the middle of quite an expanse of water, and with the enemy occupying all the surrounding islands, escape was impossible.[132]

The practical implications for any potential escapees from the Changi camp were well known to the inmates. Those that attempted to escape on the eve of the surrender generally did not succeed in eluding the concentration of Japanese naval vessels in the Java Sea. Certainly by September 1942 the Japanese were in firm control of the whole region, rendering escape even less likely. This factor alone would seem to mitigate against standing upon the issue of a 'right to escape' as being a realistic proposition. Although more than a few men did escape and successfully linked up with Chinese guerillas at large on the Malayan mainland, most were recaptured and, surprisingly, many were not shot.[133] Major Gillies went so far as to declare that 'I have not the slightest thought of attempting to escape . . . it is pure folly to even think of it as things are . . .'[134] The testimony of these men would seem to confirm the idea that, whatever the real reason for resisting the Japanese demands, a belief in escape itself was not what motivated the 17,000 men to endure three days at Selerang. The signed declaration forms bore every conceivable allegiance and *nom de plume*, with innumerable 'Ned Kellys' being the principal contribution from the AIF. The fact that the Japanese abstained from maintaining accurate lists of prisoners' names and ranks contributed to the futility of the exercise. There was no way to check accurately who had, or had not signed, nor even whether soldiers signed their correct names.

The move back into the familiar surroundings outside the Selerang area prompted many diarists to comment favourably on their return to conditions that now seemed positively comfortable. C Coombs wrote, 'Returned to 3 block in Changi, it was just like home again after those three horrible days'.[135] Flying Officer Dodds wrote 'Home sweet home! back in our old quarters at no. 47, what a relief!'[136] For these men the mere contrast of experiences was sufficient to cheer their spirits, if only temporarily. For J W Franks the return to normal prisoner accommodation was somewhat less happy. Upon their return, Franks and his comrades found their quarters had been thoroughly looted in their absence.[137]

Conclusions

For five days in 1942, 17,000 Allied prisoners of war refused to sign what they believed was an 'unreasonable' declaration. What did they hope to gain? Escape itself was virtually impossible and considered to be so by all concerned. Although the forms were eventually signed the inadequate records maintained by the Japanese, in tandem with the preponderance of false names used by the POWs, combined to render the whole exercise futile. The key to identifying the significance of the 'Selerang Barrack Square Incident' lies not in the resistance itself, although this had a profound effect on morale, but rather when exactly the POWs deigned to sign. Much was made of the change in circumstance that the 'Military Order' conferred on the situation. 'We can sign with honour,' 'Black Jack' Galleghan told his men. However, as has been seen the POWs themselves believed that any promise exacted under duress was worthless. Major Gillies asserted that 'as it is most probably a matter of threat and force . . . it does not, in my opinion mean a thing'.[138] This important 'force' criterion was satisfied by being confined within the barrack square in appalling conditions. What is equally clear is that the Japanese determination to see the forms signed had nothing to do with wanting a genuine pledge, what they sought was a pretence to deal with prisoners in a summary and in all probability brutal fashion. Whether the POWs were coerced, or signed freely, was immaterial to the Japanese as the forms themselves were worthless. Galleghan and Holmes faced a catch-22 situation with the Japanese prepared to go to any lengths to see the forms signed and the POWs obliged either to give in weakly or adopt the moral high ground, asserting that the parole was invalid because of the methods adopted to obtain a

A general view of Selerang Square, with the latrines in the foreground, September 1942. AWM Neg. No. 042303

signature. Either option would have had a disagreeable, negative impact on morale. Thus for Galleghan and Holmes the only way to secure a positive benefit from such a situation was to extract some kind of concession from the Japanese. What Galleghan referred to as 'honour' was not honour *per se* but rather an acknowledgement that the POWs had succeeded in forcing a compromise, even though had they signed earlier the ramifications would have been identical. Although the significance of such a 'victory' would appear to be essentially trivial, the practical effect upon POW morale was undeniable. This inevitably gives rise to the questions: what motivated such a course of action, and why was it so important to be seen to have won a concession from the Japanese? Changi was a comparatively 'soft' prison camp, and never approached the levels of brutality that were routine along the line of the Burma-Thailand railway. Changi remained a place to which many men were only too grateful to return following the privations and squalor experienced in Thailand.[139] This was in part a consideration, but the overwhelming factor motivating the men at Selerang may be seen to have been the humiliating defeat at Singapore. Sir Richard Sharp affirmed what most diarists only suggest when he wrote that 'we had lost a part of our self-respect with the capitulation'.[140] The comparatively unrestricted nature of Changi exacerbated the feelings of impotence and inadequacy that so many soldiers experienced. The comments from Captain Ledingham also serve to lend credence to the idea that under-performance during the Malayan campaign was a significant factor in the POWs' determination, not just to pay lip service to resisting an 'unreasonable' demand but to secure some visible sign that their resistance made an impact upon the Japanese. The fact that it was only at Changi that the parole forms were protested in such a vigorous manner also emphasises this idea. Perhaps Ledingham's incredulity may be partly explained by his role as a medical officer. Ledingham's need to reaffirm a notion of being a soldier would necessarily be somewhat different from that of front-line combat troops.

For the men at Selerang their contribution to the war effort had been little up to this point. Although the events in the square did not trouble the Japanese unduly they had a profound effect on the prisoners concerned. Generally, it would seem the men at Selerang came away with a renewed sense of belief in themselves, their units and their comrades. The practical effect was a considerable and recognisable boost in morale, manifested in a return to army discipline, all component elements of being seen to be soldiers again. When one considers that for a great many POWs the future meant only the desperate privations of the Burma-Thailand railway, one can only guess at the real impact of what these men achieved at Selerang.

No. ....

I, the undersigned, hereby solemnly swear on my honour that I will not, under any circumstances, attempt escape.

Signed

Dated

At

Nationality

Rank or Position

Selerang Declaration Form. **Appendix I**

COPY OF SELERANG SPECIAL ORDER No.3 DATED 4th.SEPTEMBER 1942.

1. On 30th.August 1942, I, together with my Area Commanders was Summoned to the Conference House, Changi Gaol, where I was informed by the represent - ative of Major General Shimpei Fukuye, G.O.C., Prisoner of War Camps, Malaya, that all Prisoners of War in Changi Camp were to be given of promise not to escape, and that all were to be given an opportunity to sign this fo-

2. By the Laws and Usages of War a Prisoner of War cannot be required by the Power holding him to give his parole, and in our Army those who become Prisoners of War are not permitted to give their parole. I pointed out this position to the Japanese Authorities.

3. I informed the representative of Major General Fukuye that I was not prepared to sign the form and that I did not consider that any Officers or men in Changi Campwould be prepared to sign the form. In accordance with the orders of the Japanese Authorities, all prisoners of war were given an opportunity to sign. The result of that opportunity is well known.

4. On the 31st.August I was informed by the Japanese Authorities that the personnel who refused to sign the certificate would be subjected to "measure of severity", and that a refusal to sign would be regarded as a direct refusal to obey a regulation which the Imperial Japanese Army considered it necessary to enforce.

5. Later, on the night 31st.August/1st.September, I was warned that on September 1st. all prisoners of war persisting in refusal to sign were to move by 1800 hours to Selerang Barrack Square. I confirmed both on my own behalf and in the name of the Prisoners of War our refusal to sign.

6. The move to Selerang Barack Square was successfully accomplished on the same afternoon.

7. I and the Area Commanders have been in constante conference with the Imperial Japanese Army and have endevoured by negotiation to have the form either abolished or at least modified. all that I have been able to obtain is, that that which was originally a demand, accompanied by threats of "measures of severity", has now been issued as an official order of the Imperial Japanese Government.

8. During the period of the occupation of Selerang Barrack Square the conditions in which we have been placed have been under my constant consideration. These may be briefly described as such, that existance therein will result in a very few days in the outbreak of epidemic and the most serious consequences to those under my command and the inevitable death of many. Taking into the low state of health in which many of us now are, and the need to preserve our force intact as long as possible, and in the full conviction that my action, were the circumstances in which we are now living known to them, would meet with the approval of His Majesty's Government, I have felt it my duty to order all personnel to sign the certificate under duress imposed by the Imperial Japanese Army.

9. I am fully convinced that His Majesty's Government only expects Prisoners of War not to give their parole when such parole is to be given voluntarily. This factor can in no circumstance be applicable to our present condition. The responsibility for this decision ~~rests with me, and with me~~ alone and I fully accept it in ordering you to sign.

10. I wish to record in this order, my deep appreciation of the spirit and good discipline which all ranks have shown during this trying period. I look to ~~y~~ all ranks to continue in good heart, discipline and morale. Thank you all for your loyalty and co-operation.

SELERANG.
4th.September 1942.

Sd/- E.B.Holmes, Colonel,
Commanding British and Australian Troops, Changi.

CERTIFIED TRUE COPY.

[signature]
Lt. Col. R. Signals.
Commanding 9/11 Ind Div Signals

Appendix II
Selerang Special Order No. 3, 4 September 1942.

COPY OF LETTER No. SELERANG 11/A of 4-9-4 .

Reference my Selerang Special Order No.3 dated 4 sep. 4 .

My attention has been drawn to some concern which is being felt that there may be adverse financial consequences on individuals as the result of the signing of the non-escape certificate.

It is obviously impossible for me to give a ruling in this matter, which must in other hands than mine, I wish, however, all ranks to be informed that this point had my full consideration at the time of the decision, and I am convinced that no such adverse consequences on pay, pension or allowances will result to any individual. It will naturally be my first endeavour, to ensure on release that the position is made clear to His Majesty's Government.

Changi. Sd/- E. B. HOLMES, Colonel,
4-9-4 . Commanding, British and Australian Troops, Changi.

Lieutenant Colonel E B Holmes's Letter No. Selerang 11/A, of 4 September 1942. **Appendix III**

Acknowledgements

The opportunity to undertake research at the Australian War Memorial was made possible thanks to a generous scholarship from the Northcote Trust.

Notes

1. Winston Churchill made this comment on hearing of Singapore's surrender; quoted in Hank Nelson, *POW, Prisoner of War, Australians Under Nippon,* Sydney, 1985, p 25.
2. After a month of captivity the Japanese ordered the prisoners to fence themselves in. Hank Nelson commented that 'some prisoners welcomed the wire. It defined themselves as well as the camp.' Hank Nelson, 'A Bowl of Rice for Seven Camels: the Dynamics of Prisoner of War Camps', *Journal of the Australian War Memorial,* No. 14, April 1989, pp 33-42.
3. 'Pinkie' Evans, The Manchester Regiment, quoted in *The Japanese Occupation: Singapore 1942-1945,* Singapore, 1985, p 26.
4. The Malayan campaign has been the subject of exhaustive discussion and innumerable books and articles. See Lieutenant-General A E Percival, *The War in Malaya,* London, 1949; Major-General S Woodburn Kirby, *History of the Second World War: The War against Japan, Volume I,* London, 1957, and *Singapore: The Chain of Disaster,* London, 1971; Louis Allen, *Singapore 1941-42,* London, 1977; and Peter Elphick, *Singapore: The Pregnable Fortress,* London, 1995, for a variety of opinions of the conduct of the campaign.
5. Louis Allen, op cit, p 125.
6. Ibid, p 121.
7. Lieutenant-General A E Percival, CB, DSO, MBE, MC.
8. Lieutenant-General A E Percival, *The War in Malaya,* London, 1949, p 110.
9. Woodburn Kirby, p 461.
10. Lord Strabolgi, *Singapore and After: A Study of the Pacific Campaign,* London, 1942, p 66.
11. Lieutenant-General Sir William Dobbie (GOC Malaya) had requested tanks from the War Office in 1937, as had his successor, General Sir Lionel Bond. See Louis Allen, p 45. None were forthcoming, however.
12. Allen, p 160.
13. Winston Churchill, quoted ibid, p 167.
14. See Major-General S Woodburn Kirby, *Singapore: The Chain of Disaster,* London, 1971, p 121, for an explanation of tactics and subsequent denials on the part of Percival.
15. Allen, op cit, p 13; also Percival, op cit, p 50.
16. For an interesting appraisal of the effect of the surrender of Singapore upon Australian morale see David Day, *The Great Betrayal: Britain, Australia and the Onset of the Pacific War,* London, 1988, pp 234-360.
17. Sergeant Jack Edwards, 155th Field Regt, Royal Artillery, The Lanarkshire Yeomanry, quoted from Edwards, *Banzai you Bastards!,* London, 1990, p 22.
18. Hank Nelson wrote that 'seeing the vast army assembled in defeat, many men could not understand why they had done so little to impede the Japanese'. 'A Bowl of Rice for Seven Camels: the Dynamics of POW Camps', *Journal of the Australian War Memorial,* No. 14, April 1989, pp 33-42.
19. Captain Grenfell Russell RN, *Main Fleet to Singapore,* London, 1951, p 64.
20. For a fuller discussion of the origins, evolution and impact of popular stereotypes of the Japanese upon the course of the Second World War, see John Dower, *World Without Mercy: Race and Power in the Pacific War,* New York, 1986.
21. Prime Minister Winston Churchill quoted in Peter Elphick, *Singapore: The Pregnable Fortress,* London, 1995, p 3. This passage is in turn quoted from Charles Eade (compiler), *Secret Session Speeches,* London 1946.
22. Lionel Wigmore, *Australia in the War of 1939-45: Volume IV, The Japanese Thrust,* Canberra, 1957, p 294.
23. General (later Field Marshal) Sir Archibald Wavell, appointed Supreme Allied Commander South-West Pacific on 30 December 1941.
24. Brian Bond (ed), *Chief of Staff: The Diaries of Lieutenant-General Sir Henry Pownall, Volume 2, 1940-1944,* London, 1973.
25. CAB 65/29 WM (42)9, 19 January 1942.
26. CABLE NO.260/2, Churchill to Wavell, 10 February 1942. Quoted in David Day, op cit, p 255.
27. IWM, MISC 1772, copy of telegram Wavell to Percival, 10 February 1942.
28. IWM, copy of Statement by Lieutenant-General Percival, 11 February 1942, reproduced in the Second World War Papers of C Wise.
29. Woodburn Kirby, *History of the Second World War,* p 324.
30. IWM, Sir Richard Sharp, 9th Battalion Royal Northumberland Fusiliers, transcript account written shortly after the Second World War, p 1.
31. Squadron Leader H A Probert, *The History of Changi,* Singapore, 1965, p 34.

32. IWM, Captain S Hannam, ms account written in 1945, p 6. This journey was an ordeal in itself. Hannam, an Australian, recalled: 'The Japs marched us 14 miles to Changi, where we arrived early next morning. We were given one cucumber and one tin of bully beef between ten men for our marching rations'.
33. Hank Nelson, *Australians Under Nippon*, p 24.
34. Basil Peacock, *Prisoner on the Kwai*, London, 1966, p 6.
35. Stan Arneil, an Australian captured at the surrender, wrote that 'it was possible to remain at Changi and rarely see a guard'. S Arneil, *One Man's War*, Sydney, 1980, pp 3-4.
36. IWM, 91/35/1, Staff Captain Sir Gilbert Inglefield, 55 Brigade, 44 pp transcript account written c 1987 based on contemporary notes, p 22.
37. Bryson collection, Royal Commonwealth Society (henceforth RCS), 'Diary of a POW, Changi, Singapore', by Lieutenant Colonel D S Ainger, ED, Armoured Car Regiment, Federated Malay States Volunteer Forces, p 10. Ainger remarks in the transcript of his contemporary journal, Part I of which was written 'during the latter half of July and early August' that 'this is not a diary . . . I wrote a spasm every three to six months'. He explains that 'in this narrative you will find the tense changing repeatedly according to whether I was writing of past or present events'. Ainger, p 1.
38. Frank Owen, *The Fall of Singapore*, London, 1960, p 12.
39. IWM, 94/4/1, E Holden, 19 pp transcript account written in 1945, p 5.
40. AWM, 54 554/11/39 AIF War Diary: Feb'42–Aug'45, pp 1-2.
41. AWM, 54 554/11/39 AIF War Diary, 1, and 554/11/4 Part 10 'Interim report on British and Australian PW Camps, Singapore Island, for period 17 Aug 42 to 31 Aug 45 by Colonel E B Holmes, MC, Comd. Brit. and Aust. Tps, Singapore', 2.
42. AWM, 3DRL 2313, 'Special Order by Maj. Gen. Callaghan', Q.1281, 20 July 1942.
43. AWM, 54 554/11/29 'Chronology of Important Events . . .', 2.
44. AWM, 54 554/11/4 Part 10, Holmes, 4.
45. Ibid, 4.
46. Ibid, 4.
47. IWM MISC. 31/Item 31, 'Selerang Declaration Form', reproduced as Appendix I.
48. Interim report by Holmes, 4.
49. Ibid.
50. Ibid.
51. Ibid.
52. AWM, 3DRL 2313, 'Barrack Square Concentration: Sequence of Events from 1-5 Sep.'
53. Ibid.
54. IWM, 81/7/1 Lieutenant Colonel C Wilkinson, 9th Battalion Royal Northumberland Fusiliers, 137 pp transcript of 3 ms diaries, entry for 2 September 1942.
55. IWM, 87/58/1, Lieutenant J A Richardson, Intelligence Corps, 89 pp transcript of ms diary, entry for Wednesday 2 September 1942.
56. AWM, PR85/145, Captain Alan W Rodgers, diary entry 3 September 1942.
57. Lieutenant Baillies thought the square to be 160×250 yards. IWM, 85/36/1, Lieutenant W H Baillies, Singapore Royal Artillery Volunteer Force, 91 pp ms diary, covering period April 1942–September 1945, entry for 30 August 1942. F G W Power believes 140×270 yards was a closer approximation. F G W Power, *Kurragh! An Australian POW in Changi, Thailand and Japan, 1942-1945*, Melbourne, 1991, p 44. Galleghan himself estimated 150×250 yards, 'Sequence of Events', 1.
58. AWM, PR00016-2, Major A N Thompson, diary entry for 2 September 1942.
59. Lieutenant Baillies, diary entry for 2 September 1942.
60. Captain Inglefield, p 33.
61. AWM, 3DRL 2313.
62. Ibid.
63. Ibid, Major Francis Magee, 21 August 1945.
64. AWM, 3DRL 2313, 'Re: Cpl Breavington and Pte Gale',1.
65. AWM, 3DRL 2313, Galleghan to Mrs R E Breavington, letter dated 3 September 1942.
66. Lieutenant Baillies, diary entry for 2 September 1942.
67. Sir Gilbert Inglefield made the following comment on these Indian 'traitors': 'In reality most of them had been forced under threat of torture and death [to change sides] so could we really blame poor bewildered Sepoys, seeing the might of Britain temporarily eclipsed and her earthly citadels for the moment crashing in ruins, for being won over by hollow words'; Inglefield, p 22. While this is partly true, the Japanese organised Indian National Army was intended specifically to fight against British rule in India.
68. E Holden, p 5.
69. Lieutenant Baillies, dairy entry for 3 September 1942.
70. AWM, 3DRL 2313, 'Sequence of Events', 2.
71. F W G Power asserts that there was in fact only a single tap in the square, op cit, pp 44-45.
72. IWM, 91/18/1, E W Whincup, sapper with 560th Field Company Royal Engineers, 42 pp transcript account based on contemporary notebook, p 10.
73. IWM, 86/67/1, J W Franks, RQMS 18th Division RASC, 81 pp account written c. 1986 covering period from 15 February 1942 to 15 August 1945, p 14. Franks also commented that 'the Singapore temperature seldom varied between 85-90 degrees'.
74. AWM, 3DRL 2313, 'Sequence of Events', 3 September 1942.
75. IWM, 8816211, Signaller C Coombs, 9 Division Signals, ms diary February 1942–October 1945, entry for 2 September 1942.
76. Lieutenant Colonel Wilkinson, diary entry for 4 September 1942.
77. Lieutenant Colonel Wilkinson, diary entry for 3 September 1942.
78. AWM, 3DRL 2313, 'Sequence of Events', 1600hrs, 3 September 1942.
79. Coombs, diary entry for 3 September 1942.
80. Lieutenant Baillies, dairy entry for 4 September 1942.
81. Imperial Japanese Army.
82. Lieutenant Colonel Wilkinson, diary entry for 4 September 1942.
83. IWM, Sharp, p 9.
84. AWM, 3DRL 2313, 'Sequence of Events', 4 September 1942.
85. Lieutenant Baillies, diary entry for 4 September 1942.
86. IWM, S Warren, Bombardier 135th Field Regiment, Royal Artillery, 20 pp transcript of ms diary, entry for 4 September 1942.
87. Lieutenant Baillies, diary entry for 5 September 1942.
88. AWM, 54 554/11/4 Part 10, Lieutenant Colonel E B Holmes, 'Interim Report . . .', 4.
89. Ibid.
90. AWM, 3DRL 2313, 'Sequence of Events', 4 September 1942.
91. Ibid.
92. Lieutenant Baillies, diary entry for 5 September 1942.
93. IWM, MISC. 147/Item 2308, Lieutenant Colonel Holmes, Selerang Special Order No. 3, 4 September 1942, reproduced at Appendix II.
94. Lieutenant Baillies, diary entry for 30 August 1942.
95. Captain Inglefield, p 31.
96. Ibid, p 34.
97. Percival, op cit, p 313.
98. Stan Arneil, *Black Jack*, p 115.
99. IWM, Lieutenant C Thornton, Subaltern, Federated Malay States Volunteer Force, transcript of contemporary ms journals written in two (49 pp and 46 pp) exercise books, p 85.
100. Captain Inglefield, p 34.
101. IWM, 84/18/1, Major D W Gillies, Royal Army Medical Corps, ms diary/journal, covering February 1942–September 1945, p 60.
102. Captain Inglefield, p 35.
103. Lieutenant Thornton, p 86.
104. Bowden, op cit, p 83.
105. Sharp, p 74.
106. IWM, Padre Noel Duckworth, '*Japanese Holiday:* a broadcast to London, 12 September 1945', transcript, p 2, held in F Smith collection.
107. Lieutenant Thornton, p 87.
108. Stan Arneil, *Black Jack*, pp 114-115.
109. Major Gillies, pp 59-60.
110. Lieutenant Colonel Wilkinson, diary entry for 4 September 1942.
111. 'Colonel Saito' from the film *The Bridge on the River Kwai*, quoted in Kate Darian-Smith and Paula Hamilton, *Memory and History in Twentieth Century Australia*, Oxford, 1994, pp 101–102.
112. Stan Arneil, *Black Jack*, p 113.
113. C Coombs, diary entry for 4 September 1942.
114. Bowden, op cit, p 89.
115. Lieutenant Baillies, diary entry for 5 September 1942.
116. E W Whincup, p 10.
117. Major Gillies, p 10.
118. C Coombs, diary entry for 4 September 1942.
119. IWM, Misc 147, Letter No. Selerang 11/A, 4 September 1942, reproduced in full at Appendix III.
120. Lieutenant Colonel E B Holmes, ibid.
121. Selerang Special Order No. 3, 4 September 1942.
122. Selerang Special Order No. 3, 4 September 1942.
123. IWM, 92/35/7, Lieutenant R J P Garden, printed memoir, p 98.
124. Gavan McCormack and Hank Nelson, *The Burma-Thailand Railway: Memory and History*, St Leonards, 1993, p 69.
125. IWM, 86/67/1 J W Franks, 'Report on the Conditions of Prisoners of War in Thailand, May to December 1943', written c. 1944 by POWs. (Copy held in Franks Collection.)
126. The *Senjinkun* or 'Combatant's Code', issued on 8 January 1941 by the Army Minister, contained the following: [that Japanese soldiers

will] not survive to suffer the dishonour of capture'. This almost certainly influenced the treatment of POWs by the Japanese. For a greater discussion of this subject see Aiko Utsumi, 'Prisoners of War in the Pacific War: Japan's Policy', in McCormack and Nelson, op cit, p 71.

127. Lieutenant J A Richardson, dairy entry for 5 September 1942.

128. Lieutenant Colonel Wilkinson, diary entry for 5 September 1942.

129. Lieutenant Baillies, diary entry for 5 September 1942.

130. IWM, Captain J Ledingham, 20 Combined General Hospital, ms diary written on the leaves of *The Albatross Book of Living Verse,* p 8.

131. Ibid, p 8.

132. E Holden, p 4.

133. See John McGregor, *Blood on the Rising Sun,* for an account of his experiences of escape from Changi and his subsequent recapture.

134. Major Gillies, p 61.

135. C Coombs, diary entry for 5 September 1942.

136. Flying Officer Dodds, diary entry for 5 September 1942.

137. Franks, p 15.

138. Major Gillies, p 61.

139. In 1980 Stan Arneil wrote: 'The portrayal of the "dreaded Changi" brings a smile to the faces of many former POWs who longed for Changi as almost a heaven on earth compared to some of the dreadful places to which they were taken'. *One Man's War,* p 3.

140. Sharp, p 4.

The National Reserve, 1910–1919

K W Mitchinson

Research into the volunteer formations raised before the Great War usually concentrates on the creation of the Territorial Force in 1908 and the Special Reserve. Only infrequent mention is made of another volunteer reserve formed in 1910 and which attracted a geat deal of contemporary interest. Created initially as the Veteran Reserve, but within a year known as the National Reserve, this at times nebulous formation boasted a strength of nearly 200,000 men. When war was declared in August 1914, many thousands of its members—former soldiers, sailors and Volunteers—flocked to the colours to offer their services to the regular, Territorial and New Armies.[1]

Mr Haldane (when Secretary of State for War) originally conceived the Territorial Force as a formation able to support the regular army on the continent in the event of war. For political reasons however, the idea that it should serve overseas was largely dropped and the force was designated for home defence. Territorial battalions had been created from the abolished Volunteer units, many of which had existed since the middle of the nineteenth century. The former Volunteers were encouraged to enlist in the new TF units, but such was the resentment at the abolition of their old battalions that many Volunteers ignored the successor units. Encouraged by an improvement in TF recruiting following the 'invasion scare' of 1909, Haldane proposed the creation of three new reserves: the TF Reserve, a Technical Reserve and the Veteran Reserve. However, with the 'scare' over, recruitment to the TF again declined, a consequence according to Haldane of 'a disease of ten years' peace'.[2] Equally important to the future of the TF was the fact that those men who had enlisted in 1908 were now approaching the end of their four year term. Haldane hoped that those

National Reserve badge, London.

K W Mitchinson has written extensively on social and military aspects of the First World War. His publications include *Gentlemen and Officers* (Imperial War Museum, 1995) and *Pioneer Battalions in the Great War* (Leo Cooper, 1997).

who were not prepared to re-enlist might commit themselves instead to a period in a reserve of some description. He told Parliament:

> We are endeavouring to organize a Veterans' Reserve, and in this connection are trying to get in each county a list of men who have served their country and passed through the Colours and Reserve, and are willing without engaging themselves to be of use in whatever way they can.[3]

A good deal of preparatory work preceded Haldane's formal acknowledgement that the Veteran Reserve had actually come into existence. Much of the credit for having turned the concept into reality lies with Mr St Loe Strachey, a JP who later became Sheriff of Surrey. His continued advocacy of the scheme did much to persuade the War Office that such an organization would be a useful adjunct to the existing auxiliary forces.

The Veteran Reserve was created by an Army Order of May 1910 and a War Office memorandum of March 1911.[4] Because it was intended to be affiliated to the TF the organization and administration was entrusted to the County Associations. From its inception, the future role of the reserve was kept deliberately vague. Haldane did not want to frighten off potential members by stipulating conditions of engagement or specifying an upper age limit. The uses to which Haldane suggested the new reserve might be put were listed as: reinforcing the regular army, to fill up existing vacancies and replace battle casualties in the TF, strengthening garrisons, guarding vulnerable points such as railways and gas works and collecting horses on mobilization.[5]

Once official sanction had been granted, most TF County Associations formed a recruiting sub-committee to cope with the anticipated enrolment of members.[6] These committees usually planned an advertising campaign, often heralded by a printed appeal from the association's president in the local press. Adverts were placed in Post Offices, police stations and cinemas, hand bills were distributed, old comrades associations contacted and addresses of former servicemen obtained from local Army Records Offices. At least one TF battalion announced that it would attach its VR units to its eight TF companies, thus providing former Volunteers with an obvious connection to their successor unit.[7]

Most adverts appealed to the virtues of patriotism and duty and stressed how the reserve would release the regulars and Territorials for more important work. Posters also frequently reiterated the army's own stated motive for creating the reserve. The *Army Annual* declared that the organization should give 'those who have served effectively and worthily in any of the military forces...a recognized and honoured position in the public life of the country'.[8] An immediate means of demonstrating this intent came with the announcement that VR members would be allowed to take part in George V's coronation parade in June 1911.

Individual counties decided how they should organize recruits once men began to register. The usual procedure was to establish companies of about one hundred men, based on towns or local or Parliamentary electoral districts. Neighbouring associations frequently came to amicable agreements about recruiting areas, but occasionally there were complaints by one county to another that it was poaching potential members.[9] The sub-committees were also generally responsible for appointing a commandant of the reserve. These men were usually former Volunteer colonels who were allowed by the War Office to retain their existing rank. Some counties used the opportunity to promote the existence of the force by offering the post of county commandant to some of the nation's foremost soldiers; others decided against appointing a commandant until the War Office issued more information about his role and responsibilities.

Within months of the scheme's beginning, most associations reported that the number of men registering was very encouraging. By July 1911 the City of London claimed that 150 men a day were signing up, while several other areas declared that hundreds had completed the enrolment form in the first few weeks. Associations were supposed to send monthly returns, but national figures were slow to be compiled. The number was high enough in June 1911 for one MP to speculate that 'in the near future' national strength could be as high as 200,000.[10] This proved to be somewhat optimistic as in February 1912 total strength was recorded as 76,000.[11] Nevertheless, by 1912 London boasted 36 battalions, organized into seven brigades.[12] By contrast, Durham was among the several counties to report that the initial response was 'disappointing', but could offer no reasons for the apparent lack of enthusiasm among its former servicemen. Similarly, West Lancashire reported that there was 'very slight progress' in its recruitment, while the annual report of the East Yorks Association noted succinctly that the 'Veteran Reserve has not prospered'. However, the majority of associations were clearly pleased with the response and were eager to maintain the momentum.

Associations quickly adopted the idea of issuing registered members with badges as a visual demonstration of a man's willingness to serve. Each county designed its own badge, the manufacture of which was often financed by wealthy benefactors. Counties were determined to exploit whatever publicity they could from the distribution of badges by organizing civic ceremonies attended by a nationally known figure. East Yorks invited Lieutenant-General Sir Herbert Plumer to present its badges and there are other similar examples. So important were the badges to members that several associations took steps to ensure that they could not be misused or transferred.

In general, the enthusiasm of former soldiers and sailors to register remained undiminished throughout 1911 and 1912. Virtually anyone who had had some sort of military service was deemed eligible for membership. Officers and men who were not members of the Reserve or liable for call up were allowed to join, as were former Special Reservists and ex-members of the Militia and Volunteers. Just about any man, of any age who was not an existing member of the TF or its reserve and who could produce a war medal to prove service, could register. Even the War Office was somewhat taken aback by the response, admitting in July 1912 that it had 'exceeded expectation'.[13] However, many associations were becoming increasingly discontented with the War Office's refusal to acknowledge the potential value of the reserve and allocate it a more specific roll. This frustration prompted the Leicestershire Association to complain that 'it seems as though not being able to do anything in peace time prevents men from joining'. Similarly the Liverpool companies were described as growing 'very impatient' about the apparent lack of War Office appreciation.

Leading from the front as usual, the Chairman of the Surrey Association insisted that the position and duties assigned to the reserve were totally unsatisfactory. He explained that the men registering were keen and enthusiastic, with 57% of them under forty. Durham also recorded that its early entrants had an average age of 39 and that 42% of them were former regulars. Lieutenant-General Elles declared that the War Office simply did not appreciate how good the material was and urged that the authorities make a definite statement on future policy so that the reservists could see in 'black and white what the intentions of the War Office were with regard to the future administration, organization and maintenance of the National Reserve'.

Numbers continued to rise from about 150,000 in August 1912 to 190,836 by the end of the year.[14] This growth coincided with the continued anxiety within the movement as to its possible use. The WO decided that it needed to know the scope of the age range of registered men before considering any more specific duties. The result of the survey showed that from a total strength of 76,972 in March 1912, just under 28,000 were officers aged between 55 and 60 and other ranks between 45 and 55. One somewhat dubious MP wondered if the Under Secretary of State knew how many were aged between 90 and 100.[15] A Leicester MP announced that there was a full battalion aged under 45 and another half battalion between 45 and 55 in his county,[16] while the City of Westminster claimed that 60% of its 36,000 members were under 42.

In the face of the continuing barrage of complaint about the lack of a more definite role, the WO became a little more receptive to suggestions made by Associations. Although it remained resolute in its determination to keep costs to a minimum, in December 1911 the WO acknowledged that the Associations' views on the liability of reservists to serve on mobilization, provision of uniform, equipment etc., would be of 'great use to the War Office Advisory Committee'.[17] It did however refuse to concede to the Associations' proposal that a proportion of the reserve should be legally bound to serve on mobilization. It also faced a new resolution that the reserve should take the place of the TF Reserve.

The TF Reserve had proved to be an abject failure but the War Office was not prepared to abandon it and replace it with the NR.[18] In an attempt to appease the associations, it despatched the Assistant Adjutant, Colonel Banon, on a whistle stop tour. Briefed to listen but to expound the official line that the NR was not intended to become a third line army, Banon travelled the counties during the summer of 1912. Exploiting contemporary concepts of a citizen army, he repeatedly stressed that the reserve would bring the army into touch with the nation by breaking down 'any prejudice that still existed against young men joining the regulars or Territorials'. By registering 'carefully, methodically and inexpensively', counties would be creating a reservoir of men with military experience into which the Adjutant-General could 'dip on mobilization'.[19]

Banon was heard with respect but his words did little to ease the frustration of the Associations. They remained very critical of the WO for its refusal to allow reservists to wear uniform and for its niggardly attitude towards musketry practise. Associations were responsible for providing uniforms to their TF members and many MPs believed that reservists should be supplied in the same way. Even a belt or a bandolier, it was suggested, would help the men to develop some sort of *esprit de corps*. The WO repeatedly rejected this suggestion, both on grounds of cost and because it considered such provision unsuitable.

Other reservists were only issued with uniforms when recalled, so to provide National Reservists with their own was considered inappropriate. Seely, the Under Secretary of State for War, also rejected the idea that members should be allowed to purchase their own uniforms.[20] Officers were permitted to wear the uniform of their former corps or regiments on civic occasions, but other ranks were entitled to wear only the buttonhole badge. This was sufficient, Seely explained, to allow men to be recognized as combatants under the Hague Convention.[21]

The provision of rifles and ammunition was an even more hotly debated topic. It was argued that if the NR was to be of any use in an emergency the men must keep up some regular rifle practice. Initially the WO announced that it might lend some rifles to companies and provide ammunition for purchase at cost price.[22] Many reservists were also members of the 140,000 strong National Rifle Association and would be able to keep up some shooting by this means.[23] Some counties established committees whose object was to raise funds for the purchase of rifles and ammunition, and in 1913 the WO agreed to supply rifles to up to 10% of the number of registered men.[24] However, it was not prepared to make money available to finance the construction of additional ranges or to supply free ammunition for men to fire a recognized course.[25] The suggestion that men be paid a retainer if they fired a certain number of shots per year was also rejected.[26] Later that same year the authorities did relent and increased the grants to Associations, largely with the intention that a proportion of the money should be spent on buying ammunition and providing transport to and from the ranges.[27]

The general issue of funding the NR was another aspect which attracted frequent discussion. On its formation the WO gave the Associations one shilling (1/-) for every registered man. This was immediately declared to be totally inadequate and in the face of extreme pressure, the WO relented and in 1913 increased the grant to 11/- for Class I, 6/- for Class II and 1/- for Class III. The distribution of the grant remained at the discretion of the Associations, but even with the increased amounts there were complaints that once administrative costs had been deducted there was little left for anything else. Although the Associations did always complain that there was inadequate funding, evidence suggests that some diverted some of the NR funds to finance their normal TF spending.[28] At least the men were assured that providing they were fit and available, their embodiment bounties would be paid by the government rather than from local funds.[29]

The classification of reservists into three classes was one of the direct consequences of Banon's troubleshooting tour.[30] Men qualifying for Class I were those under 42 whose physical fitness was sufficient for them to join a combatant unit. Class II were officers and senior NCOs under 55 and men under 50 who were fit enough for home service units. Class III were men who were qualified by age for I or II but who declined from making any definite obligation to serve, and those who were too old for the other classes. Once classification was complete, it became obvious that only about one quarter of the nearly 200,000 members were thought to be of any real military value. Seely reported to the House that there were 13,765 men in Class I and 45,722 in Class II.[31] The great majority of reservists were thus Class III and generally thought to be of little use.

The WO specified the number of men that each county would be expected to provide from Classes I and II to fill up existing vacancies in the regular army and TF. The anticipated excess number of Class II men would be used to create protection companies on mobilization to guard vulnerable points. County returns showed that the majority of Associations had insufficient men to fill up the existing vacancies, let alone have sufficient additional members to create the extra units required to guard railways and other sites. Nevertheless, Haldane insisted that the NR was a 'recognized...part of the forces of the Crown'.[32] Seely had faith in its potential, declaring it would be 'extremely valuable in maintaining lines of communication',[33] and that it was a 'military asset of the greatest value'.[34] Their opponents wondered how something that had no organization, no specified role and was comprised of men who had given no firm guarantee of service could be considered an integral part of the Crown's forces. In the House, Major Stanley agreed that the men might be 'excellent' material but criticised Seely for suggesting that they could be of any possible military value.[35] Seely was in an invidious position. He combined his office of Under Secretary of State with that of the commandant of Derbyshire's NR. While appreciating the impatience of the associations, he was unable to provide the sort of reassurance about the reserve's future that even his own county sought. When he was more forthcoming about its possible use he was roundly condemned for suggesting that the NR and the Special Reserve, 'old sweats' who knew every trick of the soldiering trade, might be put with raw recruits to bolster the regular or TF battalions. This proposal was described by one MP as 'perfectly ludicrous'.[36] Another informed the House that a senior TF officer had told him 'Heaven help us!' if the NR and Special Reserve were used to fill the ranks of the Territorials.[37]

Several battalions repeatedly demanded of the authorities what they would be expected to do on mobilization. However, as an indication of how little the WO had been prepared to contemplate a real role for the reserve, three days after the declaration of war the new Under Secretary, Mr Tennant, told the House that a review of how it might best be used was under way.[38] Given the reluctance of authority to commit itself to allocating to the reserve specific duties, it is not surprising that many members did not wait to be called. Instead they simply enlisted in their local TF or New Army battalions. Some of them were immediately transfered to the regulars and shortly found themselves being drafted to France as reinforcements for casualties sustained during the Retreat and the Battle of the Marne. Those who enlisted before they were called sacrificed their £10 bounties. Later, strenuous efforts were made on their behalf to get their gratuities paid.

By the end of August official call up of certain men had begun. Ex-regulars and NCOs of Classes I and II under 42 were enlisted into the New Armies as NCOs and all reservists of those two classes under 42 were called into Reserve units.[39] Two weeks later eligible men taken from Classes II and III were enlisted into TF units as supernumeraries. Often at the instigation of their own association, these men were equipped with whatever armbands and obsolete weapons might be available and were formed into companies to guard vulnerable points. This work could bring with it dangers. Captain Ewing, the commander of the Rye company, was killed by a train while guarding Martello Tunnel outside Folkestone Harbour.[40] Employment of NR men released TF men from these duties and allowed them to spend their time training. By late November, Tennant told the House that the call up of the NR was almost complete as the 'majority' of Classes I and II had enlisted.[41]

Despite what the Under Secretary told the House, the WO was concerned that many Class II men had either not yet presented themselves for service or were being employed inefficiently. It acknowledged that the system could not yet cope with enlisting all of the Class II men into the TF protection companies, but insisted that where vacancies did exist, preference should be given to NR men over civilian or other recruits who refused to take the general service liability. Associations were instructed to write to all registered Class II reservists who had not yet enlisted, warning them that the WO might soon withdraw the gratuity from those who delayed unnecessarily. The men were to be informed that there would be room, in most cases, for them to enlist in their own or neighbouring units and were instructed not to abandon their civilian employment until they had actually attested. Another letter was to be sent to Class II men who had not yet been used. They were ordered to obtain a medical certificate and warned that they would probably be called when the army was in a position to raise more home service TF

The Lord Mayor of London with General Corbett watching the National Guard drilling outside the Guildhall, 2 January 1915. Q 53542

The Wandsworth Home Defence Battalion was typical of the units which sprang up after the declaration of war. They attracted many Class III National Reservists. Cycle despatch riders, many wearing what are probably NR buttonholes, pose for the camera in November 1914. Q 53425

units.[42] A further letter ordered that reservists employed by firms working on government contracts and those working directly for the government would not be required to attest.[43]

By the time this latest WO letter was circulated, many NR men had already been overseas and had returned with wounds or frostbite. Three companies of the Huddersfield battalion came from the Pennine community of Saddleworth. Hardly renowned as an area of martial tradition, it produced a surprising 227 registered men from a total population of about 12,000. In August many of these immediately joined their local TF battalion, the 7/Duke of Wellington's, while others were drafted out to the 2/Duke's. Initially only those under 35 were allowed to enlist. The first 80, several of whom were South African War veterans, travelled to Huddersfield to collect kit and equipment in mid-September. By May 1915 nine of these men had been killed and at least another 20 invalided home.[44]

For those reservists who for one reason or another had not enlisted, the winter of 1914-15 and the following spring was a period of frustration. They paraded weekly, sometimes with the local reserve TF units, or more commonly with the Civilian Defence Corps. By early 1915 many counties were beginning to form what was shortly to be known as the Volunteer Training Corps from their unused Class II and Class III men. From time to time these units were ordered to parade alongside larger assemblies of unused NR men,TF and Yeomanry units. Although unrecognized by the War Office, 'hundreds, if not thousands' of reservists were reported to be on parade every Sunday on Wandsworth Common.[45] There continued to be repeated calls for the NR to be uniformed, but the authorities maintained that as there was no intention of their becoming combatants, there was no need to provide a uniform. Their somewhat motley appearance on parade led one observer to liken them to a 'body of strikers'.[46] In order to distance themselves from any such misunderstanding, members of the Huddersfield battalion were requested to wear a bowler hat when on parade.[47]

Those members who were actually in uniform and serving in the supernumerary companies of the TF believed that there were moves afoot in early 1915 to amalgamate them into a separate corps. This raised the possibility of perhaps their being transferred from a unit in which they had deliberately enlisted or even from one in which they had done their original military service.

Questions were raised in the House and for the time being the WO denied there was any intention of forming a new distinct corps.[48] Besides anxiety over this unwelcome rumour, there was continuing disquiet in several units, including those Class I reservists of the Hornsey NR attached to the 7th Reserve Battalion of the Middlesex Regiment, over the non-payment of their bounty.[49] The matter of the bounty was eventually resolved, but in late 1915, as part of the policy of reorganizing reserve and training units, the NR ceased to have a separate existence.

In the summer of 1915 volunteers from the NR serving in the supernumerary companies were sought to serve in seven new TF battalions.[50] Men had to be below 44 years of age and fit enough for garrison duties overseas. These battalions all went abroad in 1916, some to India and the remainder to the Middle East and the Balkans. The units formed at Halton Park in August 1915 and were initially known, rather clumsily, as Foreign Service TF Provisional Battalions. They included Territorials from just about every regiment of the British army. As neither the Guards and the KRRC, nor the Rifle Brigade had any direct Territorial attachments (and thus had never had NR affiliated to them), the WO decided that the battalions should be adopted by the Rifle Brigade. To substitute for the absence of any Rifle Brigade TF Association, the City of London Association agreed to assume responsibility for their administration.[51]

Those reservists who either did not volunteer for overseas service, were over age or medically unfit were gradually absorbed into the Volunteer Training Corps or the Provisional battalions then being formed for coast defence. Some months later most of the Provisional battalions were disbanded and those reservists who were still in uniform and of suitable age and of the required medical category were merged into the Royal Defence Corps. This corps was established by Royal Warrant in March 1916[52] and by the end of the war consisted of over 500 Protection Companies. In a further reorganization of August 1917 the existing Home Service Garrison Infantry Battalions were renumbered as battalions of the RDC. There were 18 of these units stationed at various ports, docks and other vulnerable points around the coast. It was in these battalions that the more elderly reservists saw out the remainder of the war.[53]

What amounted to obituaries for the NR were already being written in late 1915.[54] Understandably, they praised the readiness of the men to serve their country and

Members of the Wandsworth Home Defence Battalion practise musketry under the instruction of a sergeant. The supply of arms of such battalions was very low government priority. These apparently matching rifles were possibly borrowed for the benefit of the camera. Q 53426

The age and attire of these members of the Wandsworth Home Defence Battalion suggest that they were probably Class III reservists from the artisan and lower middle class. They were possibly a mixture of ex-regulars, former members of Volunteer Battalions or early Territorials. Q 53418

the concept of the NR as a whole. There were still many at home, although over 50, who were hoping that their military experience might be put to more use than the local VTC. Some might have eventually enlisted in the RDC, but the majority had to be content with the uniform and equipment of the VTC. While they guarded home utilities, POW camps and coastal defences, the reservists in the RDC were usually out of immediate danger. Nevertheless, over 600 members of the RDC died while on active service.[55] Thirty-one of them went down with the mail steamer *Leinster* when she was torpedoed in the North Sea in October 1918, but the majority of these sometimes elderly warriors died of natural causes.[56] Their usually younger and more active comrades who died overseas were frequently victims of some tropical disease. Before the armistice in Europe came into effect, the seven Rifle Brigade battalions containing large numbers of former reservists sustained 205 fatalities. Although 39 were drowned when the *Ivernia* went down in the Mediterranean, the great majority of these men died of disease. At least another 40 died before the battalions were finally brought home from places such as Burma, India and the Andaman Islands in 1919.[57]

Because so many members joined up before being called and were therefore not always listed as registered reservists when enlisting, it is impossible to compute precisely the number of Class I and Class II men who died on active service. Seven of the 40 Rye members were killed[58] and at least a dozen from the Saddleworth companies also fell.[59] The total national figure would undoubtedly run into several thousands. The enthusiasm with which these and the nearly 200,000 others who registered offered their services typified the Edwardian ideals of patriotic duty and self-sacrifice. Remaining for some years in ignorance as to how their experience might be utilized, and also prepared to spend their own money to maintain some degree of military fitness, National Reservists deserve to be remembered alongside those of the other voluntary forces who performed such valuable, if largely unsung work during the Great War.

Wearing the uniform of his former regiment and his NR armband, an elderly National Reservist supervises troops recently arrived on a leave train at a London terminus. Q 30513

Notes

1. A more expansive discussion by the author on the creation of the NR and the wartime experience of its successor units will be published in 1998.
2. *Hansard* 1911, 241.
3. Ibid, 229.
4. Army Order 21 May 1910 and WO Memo No.324.
5. National Reserve Regulations, 1911.
6. Unless otherwise stated, the detail comes from the TF County Association Minute Books. The majority of these records is held by County Record Offices. Unfortunately, a significant number of these books has disappeared.
7. The 10/Manchester, the Oldham Territorial battalion.
8. *Army Annual*, 1911, p 267.
9. For example, the Cheshire Association complained that men of the Liverpool NR were parading on the Cheshire side of the Mersey.
10. *Hansard* 1911, 925.
11. *Hansard* 1912–13, 486.
12. In June 1912 the King reviewed over 19,000 of the City of Westminster's NR in a huge parade held in Hyde Park.
13. WO letter to Nottinghamshire TF Association.
14. I F Beckett, *The Amateur Military Tradition, 1858–1945*, MUP, p 222.
15. *Hansard* 1912–13, 506.
16. Ibid, 1046.
17. Conference of NR commandants at the WO, December 1911.
18. The strengths of the TF Reserve are not frequently minuted by the Associations. Some examples are: City of London, 5 officers and 5 men (Oct 1910), Bucks, 3 officers (1913), Derbyshire, 6 officers and 38 men (July 1913).
19. Banon's discussions with the County Associations were often minuted in some detail. Local papers usually carried reports of his meetings.
20. *Hansard* 1914, 175.
21. *Hansard* 1911, 990.
22. *Army Annual* 1911, p 268.
23. *Army Annual* 1912, p 20.
24. *Hansard* 1912–13, 1066.
25. Ibid, 1113.
26. *Hansard* 1913, 298.
27. Ibid, 537.
28. The evidence is scanty but, for example Hereford & Worcester seem to have made a profit of £112 on its NR account in 1914 and East Yorks, £361. By contrast, West Lancs NR had overspent by £228 and asked the County Association to bail it out.
29. On mobilization Class I reservists would receive £10 and their Class II comrades £5.
30. National Reserve Regulations, 1913.
31. *Hansard* 1914, 92.
32. National Reserve Regulations, 1913.
33. *Hansard* 1914, 158.
34. *Hansard* 1912–13, 283.
35. *Hansard* 1914, 310.
36. *Hansard* 1913, 76.
37. Ibid, 626.
38. *Hansard* 1914, 1375.
39. War Office circular, 9/9/14 WO95,162/3.
40. L A Vidler, *The Story of the Rye Volunteers*, Rye Museum Committee, p 72.
41. *Hansard* 1914–15, 642.
42. WO circular to TF Association, 21/12/14 WO95 162/3.
43. WO circular to TF Associations, 14/12/14 ibid.
44. K W Mitchinson, *Saddleworth 1914–1919: The Experience of a Pennine Community during the Great War*, Saddleworth Historical Society, 1995.
45. *Hansard* 1914–15, 417.
46. *Hansard* 1914, 182.
47. *Saddleworth & Mossley Reporter*, 19 July 1914.
48. *Hansard* 1914–15, 515. For a lengthy discussion on the Parliamentary controversy surrounding the transfer of one regiment to another, see K W Mitchinson, *Gentlemen and Officers*, IWM,1995.
49. *Hansard* 1914–15, 1645.
50. The battalions were later given titles which accorded roughly to the Territorial origins of the National Reservists from which they were raised. For example, the 18th (London) Battalion took reservists largely from the London Regiment, the Queen's, Sussex, Middlesex, etc.
51. No officers of the Rifle Brigade were appointed to these battalions.
52. The Royal Warrant was followed by WO authorization by ACI No.841 of 1916.
53. The War Diary of the 12th Battalion RDC (WO95 5460) notes that on its formation in August 1917 the unit's four companies were to undertake the same duties as the unit from which it sprang, the 5th Battalion Royal Welsh Fusiliers. It had two companies at Liverpool and two at Barrow. Its strength amounted to about 1,200 men over 41 years, classified as B2 and C2.
54. Although the NR officially ceased to exist, local papers reported shooting competitions between 'NR' and VTC teams well into 1916.
55. *Soldiers Died in the Great War*, Part 77.
56. Members of the corps who died on active service were entitled to an Imperial War Graves Commission headstone.
57. *Soldiers Died in the Great War*, Part 74.
58. Vidler, op cit, p 72.
59. K W Mitchinson. *Saddleworth 1914–1919.*

Interned by Nazi Germany: a record in snapshots

Hilary Roberts

The internment of civilians from Britain and elsewhere by Germany during the Second World War is a subject for which very little documentary or published information exists. It is also an aspect of the War to which professional war photographers were denied access. However a collection of amateur photographs, held by the Photograph Archive at the Imperial War Museum, offers a source of information to researchers as well as a fascinating example of the valuable contribution which amateur photographers can make to the historical record.

The collection, which was assembled through the generosity of former internees, consists of more than a hundred snapshots showing life and events at Ilag Liebenau, an internment camp for women and children near Lake Constance in Germany, during the War. The quality of the images naturally varies considerably and the choice of subject reflects the fact that photography could only take place with the permission of the German authorities. However the collection is a remarkably candid record which warrants serious attention.

The outbreak of the Second World War in 1939 presented the German authorities with the problem of what to do with some 2,000 British subjects who had been either unable or unwilling to leave Germany before the frontiers closed. Initially, only men of military age were interned. The remainder were required to report regularly to the police. A few were allowed to leave via a neutral country, but the majority remained and their numbers increased to more than 3,000 following Hitler's conquest of Western Europe in 1940. At this point, a policy of mass internment was introduced and it was established that Germany would only repatriate civilians on an exchange basis.

Those who were interned were, in effect, prisoners in Germany. Equipped with one small suitcase of possessions each, the civilian internees were confined to strictly supervised detention camps. Few of the inmates posed a major risk to German national security and the German authorities were mindful of the large number of their own civilians in British hands. The treatment of internees therefore differed dramatically from that meted out to prisoners of war or political prisoners held in Germany. A post-war report by the Prisoners of War Department of the British Foreign Office states that the German authorities could not:

> be accused of brutal or even harsh treatment towards British subjects, except under very exceptional circumstances.[1]

Hilary Roberts is Head of Collections Management in the Photograph Archive, Imperial War Museum

Ilag Liebenau, c. 1941. HU 48361

The original inmates of Liebenau. Nuns and some of the few remaining mentally handicapped patients at work in the convent garden, c. 1941. HU 48372

A birthday party for one of the internees. The daughter of the founder of the Salvation Army, Mary Bramwell Booth, is standing towards the back on the right. HU 48409

Internees receive a consignment of Red Cross parcels, 1941. Such parcels were vital in ensuring that internees did not suffer serious deprivation. HU 48418

On the contrary, Germany:

> accepted some measure of responsibility for their maintenance, although this tended to be limited, in a lesser or greater degree, to the provision of shelter, bedding and standard rations.[2]

Liebenau, a well endowed convent surrounded by an extensive estate of farmland, had also functioned as a residential home for the aged and mentally handicapped before the war. Although the Catholic Sisters and some of their patients remained at Liebenau after the outbreak of war, space was created by the removal (probably to an unpleasant fate) of the severest cases. This was converted to serve as an internment camp for women and children. The camp differed from other German internment camps in that it was administered by the civil police rather than the military authorities (a concession to a low risk category of prisoner) and that much day to day management of the accommodation was undertaken by the nuns.

In October 1940 the first party of internees was transferred to Liebenau from Germany, Czechoslovakia and Poland. It was followed by a large group from the Netherlands in early 1941. The camp expanded yet further when the United States entered the war in December 1941 and from then until the end of the war held more than 300 women and children in very overcrowded conditions. The internees were mostly citizens of Britain or America. However this apparent commonality disguised a multitude of differing backgrounds, languages and customs. Many had either acquired citizenship through marriage, been born abroad of a British father or came from countries under British or American protection. Their links with the country named on their passports could best be described as tenuous. In the circumstances therefore, their achievement in organising themselves into an effective and cohesive group soon after their arrival was considerable.

From the start, the women of Liebenau did their best to record the experience of internment on film. They were equipped only with those personal cameras which they had been able to take with them into captivity. Like many amateur photographers in more normal circumstances, they generally concentrated on those events and aspects of life which gave them pleasure and which broke the monotony of daily existence. The effect, at a

German guards at Liebenau. Note the blackboard which announces an afternoon walk for internees outside the camp, c. 1941. HU 48423

Internees wearing costumes which they had made out of paper for a camp entertainment, 6 June 1941. HU 48393

Glamour could survive internment. An internee from Poland. HU 48395

superficial level, is to suggest that life as an internee at Liebenau was in fact rather good. Such material reflected well on the Germans, who gained an opportunity for favourable propaganda by permitting it and, until the course of the war turned against them, facilitated the production of numerous copies as souvenirs.

The internees were necessarily selective in what they photographed. They operated under severe restrictions and had limited supplies of film at their disposal. They had little to gain and much to lose by photographing contentious subjects. Nevertheless they still sought, subtly, to convey the reality of their situation. Evidence of the stress and suffering of internment is clearly detectable in many apparently innocent snapshots of smiling faces.

In truth, it was not so hard for the internees to smile at first. As the Foreign Office noted after the war:

> Once they had accustomed themselves to the initial loss of freedom, interned civilians were in some respects better off than those who were left uninterned . . . [they] had not the daily problem of finding food, clothing and work . . . and w[ere] unlikely to be suspected of subversive activities.[3]

Anita Feuerheerd, an internee and one of the contributors to the Museum's photographic record, confirmed in an interview that:

> . . . on the whole we were really quite a happy crowd . . .[4]

Initially, Red Cross inspectors from neutral countries visited reasonably regularly and regarded

Interned children and their teachers in the schoolroom at Liebenau. HU 56335

Internees working in the laundry. An aspect of daily life at Liebenau which the camera struggles to capture. HU 48412

Inspector Thoma, the Gestapo officer responsible for Liebenau, c. 1941. HU 48382

Liebenau as a model camp.[5] Most internees depended on supplies of food, clothing and money from the Red Cross for survival. In vivid contrast to the experiences of Allied prisoners of war, the Germans generally delivered such supplies promptly and without restriction. The photographs confirm the importance of such supplies in preventing serious deprivation at the camp. On a more frivolous note, the numerous photographs of flattering outfits prompt the conclusion that, during the first years of confinement at least, conditions were sufficiently comfortable to permit a feminine interest in clothes to prevail at Liebenau.

The good conditions, the family circumstances of many of the internees and the increasing uncertainties of life outside the camp ensured that there were very few attempts to abscond from Liebenau. Contact with the outside world was therefore occasionally permitted by the German authorities during the early years. The photographs record walks in the countryside surrounding Liebenau during good weather and a visit by a party of journalists from the (then neutral) United States to inspect conditions in early 1941. But above all, the photographs record the spirit and ingenuity of the internees themselves in using their own resources to keep boredom and consequent demoralisation at bay. Photographs of small celebrations, educational classes, craftwork and amateur dramatics are the single most important element of the

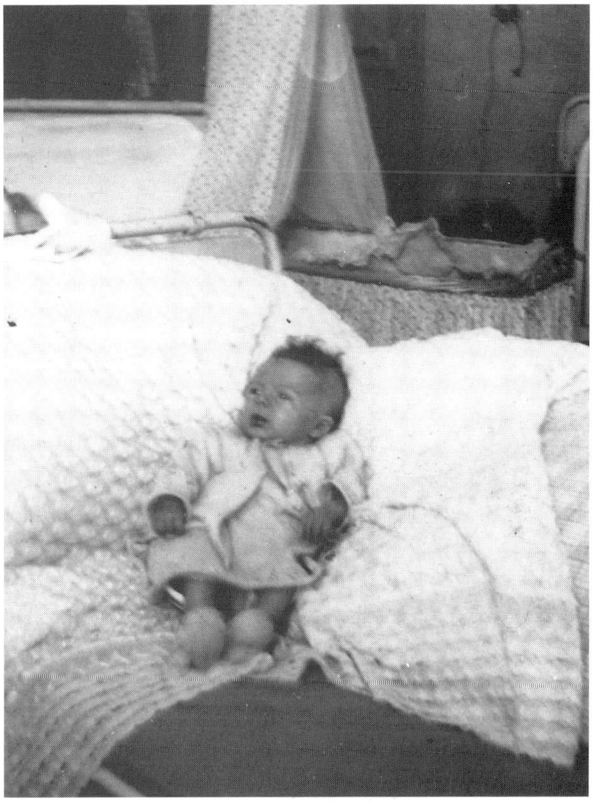

A mute witness to personal tragedy. One of the photographs of the baby girl born into internment at Liebenau, 1941. HU 48432

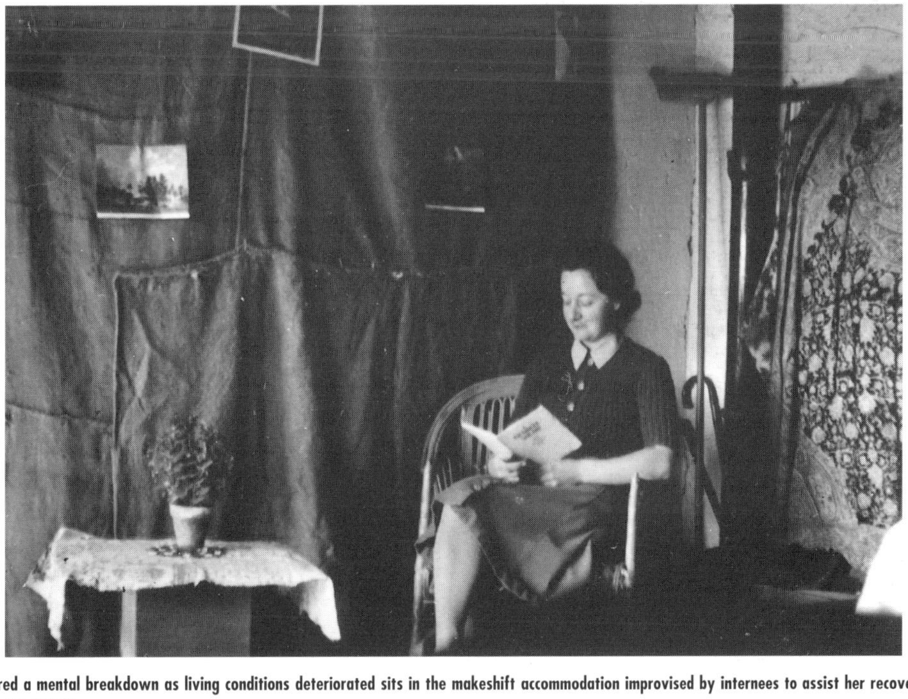

An internee who suffered a mental breakdown as living conditions deteriorated sits in the makeshift accommodation improvised by internees to assist her recovery. She was eventually repatriated. HU 48447

Confinement. The reality of internment for the women and children of Liebenau. HU 56330

Internees confined to the church crypt at Liebenau as a reprisal following the Dieppe Raid in August 1942. HU 48442

collection and naturally contribute to the overall impression of favourable conditions.

However, the internees also tried to capture the routine aspects of internment. Here they were hampered by their equipment as well as the restrictions imposed by the Germans. The internees' simple box cameras were best suited to outdoor photography in good light and this inevitably limited coverage. But there are enough images to give a clear impression of living conditions and the daily chores. Their captors, rather homely looking groups of German policemen, feature in the collection as does a portrait of the Camp's altogether more sinister looking Gestapo officer. More attractive subjects are the nuns, to whose kindness and efforts to alleviate living conditions the internees owed a great deal.

In spite of the determined cheerfulness of much of the photography, the bleaker aspects of internment are implicit in the collection from the earliest days. Mute witnesses to personal tragedy are the photographs of a baby girl born in Liebenau. Her parents had been rescued from a torpedoed passenger ship by the Germans and her father accidentally shot dead by a panicking guard. Her mother, unaware that she was pregnant, was transferred to Liebenau where the baby was born in October 1941. All the internees attended the christening, in which Mary Bramwell Booth, the daughter of the founder of the Salvation Army, participated.

By the end of 1942 the tide of war was turning against Germany. There was a corresponding deterioration in conditions at Liebenau and relations between the internees and their captors worsened. Opportunities for photography decreased as more restrictions were imposed and the supply of film ran low. The record of these mounting problems is therefore very limited. What is perhaps hardest to determine from those photographs which were taken is the effect of the prevailing conditions on relations between the internees themselves. According to the few contemporary accounts which exist, mounting stress caused the bonds between these women of very mixed origin to begin to disintegrate. An internee who was repatriated in 1943 and soon after published her experiences in a series of newspaper articles, described Liebenau as having '. . . this petty atmosphere of hysterical, neurotic women . . .'[6]

The post-war report on Liebenau by the Prisoners of War Department of the Foreign Office states that by May 1943:

> . . . much discontent and ill-natured gossip, the result of living in such cramped quarters, had produced a most unhappy atmosphere . . .[7]

Very little of this is evident in the photographs. What does feature is the effort made by internees to help one woman who suffered a breakdown and needed special accommodation. Also recorded is the tragedy of one elderly internee in frail health, whose death was a direct consequence of the poor conditions.

In comparison to the inmates of prisoner of war camps and concentration camps in Germany, it cannot be argued that the internees suffered serious mistreatment. However they did manage to photograph the most serious example, which occurred following the raid by Allied forces on Dieppe in August 1942. The Germans believed that the Allies had mistreated German prisoners captured during the raid and accordingly punished Allied prisoners of war and internees held throughout the Reich. At Liebenau eighty women were confined to the church crypt every night for weeks in cramped and overheated conditions. In the words of Anita Feuerheerd:

> It was difficult to sleep of course . . . it's so restless, completely restless, the feeling you couldn't breathe down there.[8]

The fact that the internees managed to photograph such treatment in detail, despite the limitations of their equipment, bears witness to the independence of their record of Liebenau.

In such circumstances and with the end of the war clearly some distance away, the attention and cameras of the internees focused on repatriation. Between 1943 and 1944, a number of internees from Liebenau were repatriated to Britain and America on an exchange basis. The last and most poignant of the internees' photographs record the departure of the few fortunate enough to be selected for repatriation, watched by those who would have to wait until the end of the war in 1945 before they too were liberated.

Any summary of the internees' photographic record of Liebenau cannot overlook the fact that it has considerable gaps in its coverage. However the collection is a genuine record and a unique witness of an experience which was beyond the reach of any professional war photographer of the time. Above all it is an example of what could be achieved by amateur photographers during the Second World War in spite of very limited resources. It confirms that historians cannot afford to ignore the work of the amateur photographer.

Repatriation. Four internees leave Liebenau for England watched by those left behind, October 1943. HU 48448

Acknowledgements

The Imperial War Museum's photographs of Liebenau were acquired by courtesy of Miss Anita Feuerheerd and Miss Elisa McIntyre, both former internees. They are catalogued under the references HU 48339—HU 48461 and HU 56330—HU 56340 and may be viewed in the Visitors' Room of the Museum's Photograph Archive. I am indebted for much of my further information on Liebenau to Miss Feuerheerd whose recorded memories may be heard in an interview held by the Museum's Sound Archive (catalogue reference 8701/11).

Notes

1. Sir Harold Satow KCMG OBE and Mrs M J See, *The Work of the Prisoners of War Department*, Foreign Office, 1950, p 81.
2. Satow and See, p 80.
3. Satow and See, p 81.
4. Imperial War Museum Sound Archive, interview with Anita Feuerheerd, IWM/8701/11/5.
5. Satow and See, p 97.
6. Mrs Peggie Paterson, 'Our German Guards with a Song', *The Sunday Chronicle*, 26 December 1943.
7. Satow and See, p 98.
8. Feuerheerd interview, IWM/8701/11/5.

Breakout from encirclement: the 2nd Motor Torpedo Boat Flotilla in the Far East, 1938–1942

L C Reynolds

In 1935 progressive boat designers produced speculative prototypes of a new type of Royal Naval craft which came to be called Motor Torpedo Boats (MTBs). They were a development of the First World War fast coastal motor boats which had been designed to operate in shallow waters close to any enemy coast. Their main operational purpose was to seek, attack and sink enemy ships, taking advantage of their speed and low silhouette to approach to short range. They could also be used in gun attacks on small patrol vessels close inshore and to lay mines.

The early MTBs were 60-foot British Power Boats, with plywood 'planing' hulls and powerful engines capable of giving 33 knots. They carried two 18-inch torpedoes, depth charges and pairs of Lewis guns mounted fore and aft.

By the time war was declared in 1939 only a handful had been built. Among those in service were the six transported to Hong Kong in 1938 to form the 2nd MTB Flotilla. The six boats were numbered MTBs 07 to 12, and the flotilla was made up to eight by the addition of two Thornycroft 55-foot boats (MTBs 26 and 27) which had originally been built for the Chinese Navy from First World War designs.

A Lieutenant Commander led the flotilla and an engineer officer and maintenance staff were attached. They received their operational orders from the Commander-in-Chief (C-in-C) China Station, through the local naval staff.[1]

All the officers of the 2nd Flotilla in Hong Kong were either young RN Lieutenants enjoying a very early taste of command, or Sub-Lieutenants appointed as their First Lieutenants, responsible for gunnery and navigation. The colonial peace-time routine of 1938–39 was shattered by the onset of war in Europe, and anxious eyes were cast at the Japanese forces who, at war with China, had landed

MTB 09 at Hong Kong, spring 1940.

L C Reynolds, a retired Headmaster, is the author of *Gunboat 658*.

only fifty miles from Hong Kong and whose domination of much of South China was a threat. By the beginning of 1940, most of the RN officers had been sent home to take up appointments in destroyers, and their places had been taken by RNVR officers from the UK or from the Hong Kong Volunteer Reserve.

The Senior Officer (SO) of the flotilla, having formed and trained it since 1938, was,however, retained to ensure continuity. Lieutenant Commander D G Clark RN was highly respected, and worked hard to bring his Reserve officers to a high level of efficiency. Each boat, in addition to its two officers, had a crew of seven composed of a Petty Officer coxswain, a Petty Officer Motor Mechanic, a stoker, a telegraphist/signalman, and three gunnery and torpedo ratings. They all lived ashore when in harbour as conditions aboard were very cramped and facilities minimal.

In Hong Kong, their duties on a war footing were largely local defence patrols, and included a constant watch on the minefields which protected the entrance to the main harbour. Later, as tension increased when the Japanese signed a Tripartite Pact with Germany and Italy in September 1940, it was necessary to patrol off the northern shore of Mirs Bay to the east of the Colony, which was Chinese territory but under Japanese control. The deep channel to the Canton River to the west was outside British waters, and was constantly used by Japanese ships which occasionally diverted to 'snoop' over the limit. The MTBs were under orders to avoid provocation and quietly to escort them away.

Piracy was not unknown in the area, and the boats were sometimes involved in seeking out Chinese pirate bands which entered British waters and attacked trading junks. On one occasion, the CO of MTB 09 was able to signal to the Commodore in Naval HQ at Victoria 'Engaging pirates ashore on north-west Lantau. Landing party investigating'. The subsequent report led to the capture of the band by the Hong Kong Police.

The great majority of the flotilla's time was spent in training exercises. In them, British ships approaching the Colony were (after warnings) subjected to mock attacks by torpedoes with dummy warheads. It was no easy task to fire torpedoes from those early MTBs: they were

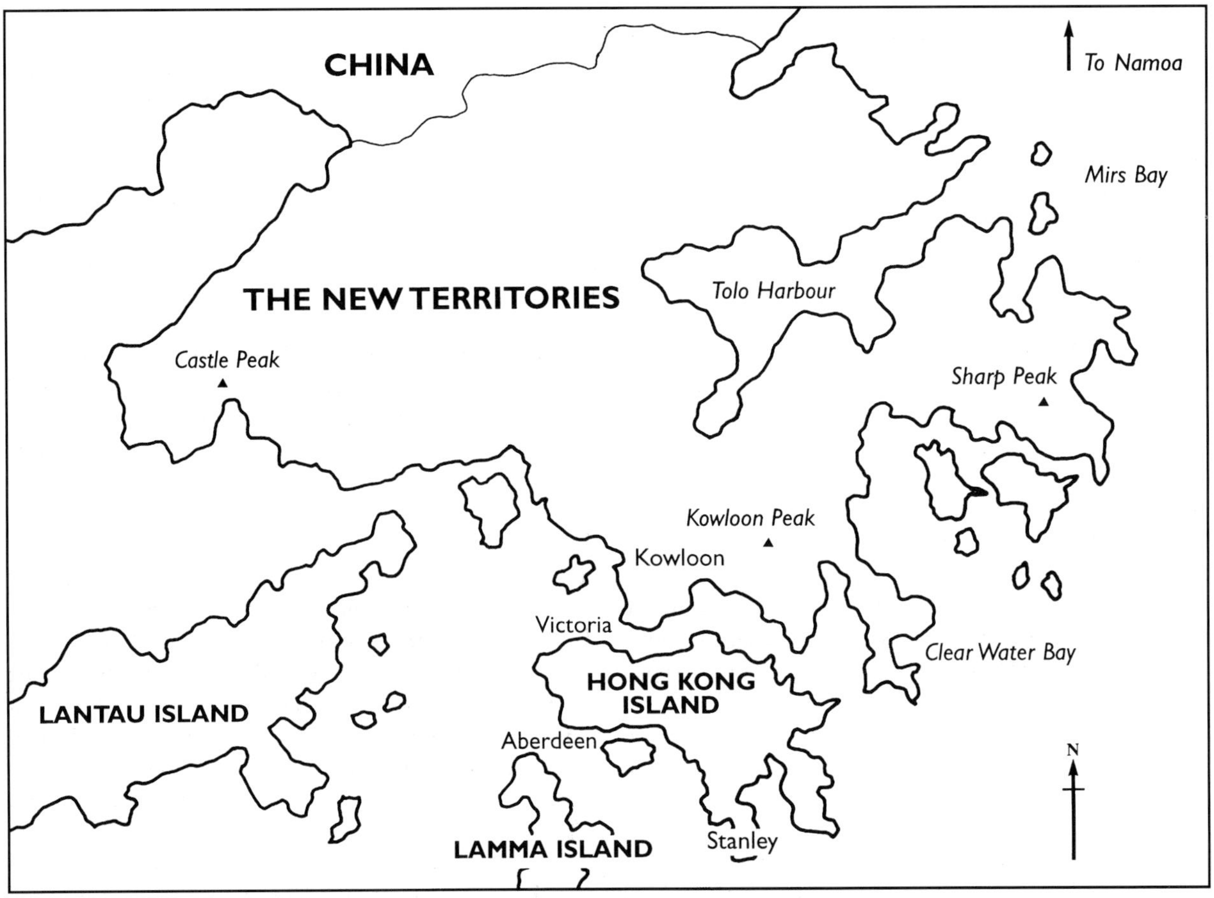

Hong Kong, the New Territories and South China.

housed at high level in the engine room, and were first propelled astern, guided by rails on a gantry projecting over the transom. Once launched, the motor took the torpedo forward, aiming in the direction in which the boat had been steering when it was fired; the boat had to accelerate away and veer off course to avoid being rammed astern. The boats practised very close station-keeping at high speed and many other manoeuvres aimed at preparing the crew for any eventuality in action.[2]

Lieutenant Commander Clark left Hong Kong in November 1940, and was succeeded by an RN Lieutenant Commander brought back from retirement and many years older than the young Reserve officers he led. Gerard Gandy had the unenviable task, as the threat of Japanese attack on the Colony increased month by month, of trying to continue the training programme, to command MTB 10, and to keep in touch with the constantly changing military and political situation.

In November 1941, as tension with Japan increased, army reinforcements arrived, and MTB patrols were stepped up. On 7 December, a signal was received by the boats: 'Commence hostilities against Japan'. News arrived of the massive raid on Pearl Harbor, and almost at once Japanese bombers began attacking Kai Tak, the airport on Kowloon Bay. The MTBs were moved from their normal berths to the little dockyard at Aberdeen on the west side of Hong Kong Island. It was essential to maintain them in serviceable state as long as possible, as by the end of that day, with two of the port's three destroyers sent to Singapore, only the third, HMS *Thracian*, the MTBs, and the river gunboat HMS *Tern* (HMS *Cicala* was at this time under repair in dock) were left to support the army in the defence of the Colony.

The enemy began their land assault from the north on 8 December, and their heavy concentrations of troops and artillery drove the army back through the New Territories day after day. Some troops were trapped close to the shores of Kowloon Bay, and the MTBs were used to evacuate them to Hong Kong Island; on one occasion each boat brought out sixty troops on each of three trips, a very hazardous operation in such small, unstable craft. On 17 December *Thracian*, now in dry dock at Aberdeen, was badly hit in an air raid and subsequently beached, and in the same attack, MTB 08 was destroyed when under repair on the slip ashore.

The MTBs were frustrated in that without any targets worthy of torpedo attack, their main function was nullified; but suddenly, soon after dawn on 19 December, there was a 'call to arms'. A signal from Naval HQ ordered all available MTBs to enter Victoria Harbour to 'attack Japanese landing craft until all ammunition expended'. At

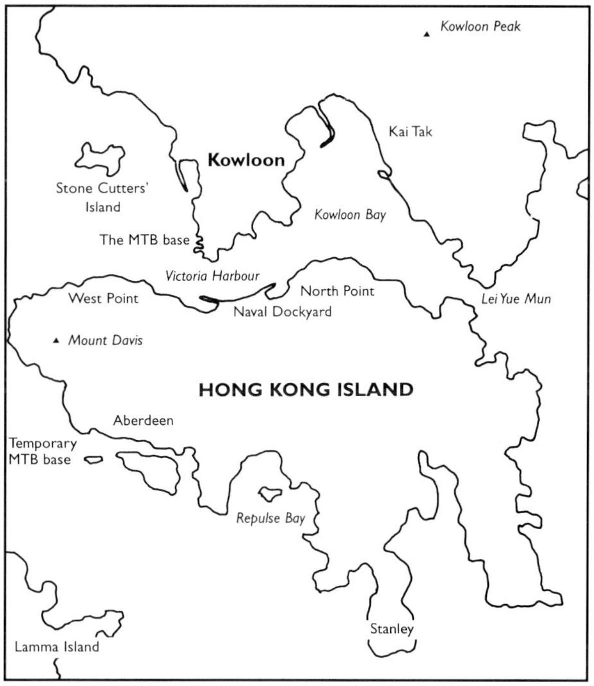

Hong Kong and Kowloon.

last, this was something aggressive to do after twelve days of being on the receiving end of bombing and machine gun attacks from aircraft.

Early that morning, Gandy received information that Japanese troops were being ferried across from Kowloon towards Taipoo on Hong Kong Island, and he immediately sent MTB 07 (Lieutenant R R W Ashby RHKNVR) and 09 (Lieutenant A Kennedy RNVR) to intercept and destroy the transports and thus frustrate the landing. As his own boat MTB 10 had engine trouble, MTBs 11 and 12 were sent to make a second attack, with 26 and 27 standing by in case a third was necessary.

Gandy's report to the C-in-C East Indies, made ultimately on 8 March 1942, in Rangoon, gives the details:

> At 0845, MTBs 07 and 09 proceeded at full speed and made a successful surprise attack on Japanese towed in flat-bottom boats, overturning them with wash, Lewis-gunning them and completely dispersing the daylight landing attempt. 07 and 09 were fired upon continuously by enemy batteries, machine guns, and from the air. 07 made two attacks and attempted to drop depth charges under the enemy, but found the water too shallow to explode them. 07 lost first one engine and then

> a second to cannon fire from aircraft. 09 attacked independently and then rejoined 07 to tow her out of the Harbour area. Two of 07's crew were killed. The boats were handled with great efficiency bringing great credit to Commanding Officers, coxswains and crews . . .[3]

As the boats left Hong Kong Harbour, MTBs 11 (Lieutenant C J Collingwood RN) and 12 (Lieutenant J B Colls RHKNVR) moved in to replace them and make further independent attacks, and at once came under heavy fire. They found that the landing attempt had been abandoned and no Japanese craft remained to attack. MTB 11 was hit and the coxswain wounded. As the boat turned to leave the Harbour area, Collingwood realised that he could see no signs of MTB 12: his crew reported they had last seen her lying stopped with clouds of white smoke around her. She had clearly been sunk, as far as they knew with no survivors. In Lieutenant Commander Gandy's report he was able to note an unconfirmed statement that MTB 12 had indeed been disabled and helpless and that the CO had ordered 'abandon ship'. One crew member (Able Seaman Bartlett) was believed to have been able to swim ashore.

A third unit, MTBs 27 (Lieutenant T M Parsons RHKNVR) and 26 (Lieutenant D W Wagstaff RHKNVR) was ordered to make a final sally into Kowloon Bay. On the way, as 27 slowed to receive a signal from the Mt Davis signal station ordering the unit to remain outside till further notice, MTB 26 shot past and entered the Harbour in execution of the original orders. She was never seen again, and was clearly another victim of either air attack or fire from the shore.[4]

There was great shock and sadness in the flotilla at having lost so many close friends and two boats in so short a time. A signal was received that afternoon from the Commodore:

> The attacks carried out by the flotilla were most gallant and an inspiration to everybody. Regret losses incurred but like you, proud of their devotion to duty.

Over the next five days the serviceable boats were kept busy on patrols and individual missions. Plans began to be made for the inevitable end as the Japanese artillery and aircraft kept up constant attacks on all the island's strong points. Gandy received orders to take aboard the boats of the flotilla three European guerrilla leaders who had already been active behind the Japanese lines. Should the surviving naval personnel be able to break out from Hong Kong through South China, they would be invaluable.

HMS *Cicala*, the last of the river gunboats (which had only just completed repairs), was sunk after bombing, and her crew taken off by MTB 10. Ammunition was ferried to Stanley to enable the battery there to fire. The boats could no longer lie in the Aberdeen Channel as it was now under direct fire from Japanese artillery, and were dispersed to await orders. By Christmas Day, with white flags flying over Hong Kong, the time had clearly come to gather the flotilla in a more distant area, but Gandy, who had been given orders to take on board 'an important Chinese personage with his staff' had not been able to make contact with that group, and held on at the rendezvous near Aberdeen Island.

He knew by now that 'the personage' was Admiral Chan Chak of the Chinese Military Mission. Communication systems were breaking down, but suddenly a swimmer was seen slowly moving towards MTB 10. He proved to be a member of the Admiral's staff. The Admiral's party was hiding on Aberdeen Island, where they had swum when the motor boat, in which they had got away just before enemy troops reached their headquarters, was machine gunned and sunk. Admiral Chan Chak had been wounded in the wrist and was further hampered by his wooden leg which he discarded with great calmness and determination as he slipped over the side to swim for Aberdeen Island. Not all the twenty-strong party in the boat made it to the shore, but the Admiral did, and half scrambling, half crawling, he managed to get round the corner of the island to find help at hand.

MTBs 10 and 27 had waited at the rendezvous, and sent a party ashore to bring the twelve survivors aboard. They were stripped of their wet clothing, and by the time the remaining boats arrived, having at last been summoned, they had just been dressed in any spare clothes the two boats could find. The Admiral, who refused to stay below, and who despite his wound looked surprisingly cheerful, was sitting on MTB 10's bridge in his new Lieutenant Commander's uniform borrowed from Gandy. He was diminutive and middle-aged, with a bright, alert face and he exuded calm and authority.

At once plans were made, with the help of the experts in guerrilla warfare, who were known to the MTB men only as 'Mike', 'John' and 'Mac'. Clearly the first tasks were to land at a point on the mainland coast free of Japanese, to destroy the boats, and to move everybody as far inland as possible before daylight revealed their trail.

The boats set out round the south coast of Hong Kong Island making for Mirs Bay to the east. They made landfall by midnight off the village of Namoa, contacted Chinese guerrillas, and landed all their

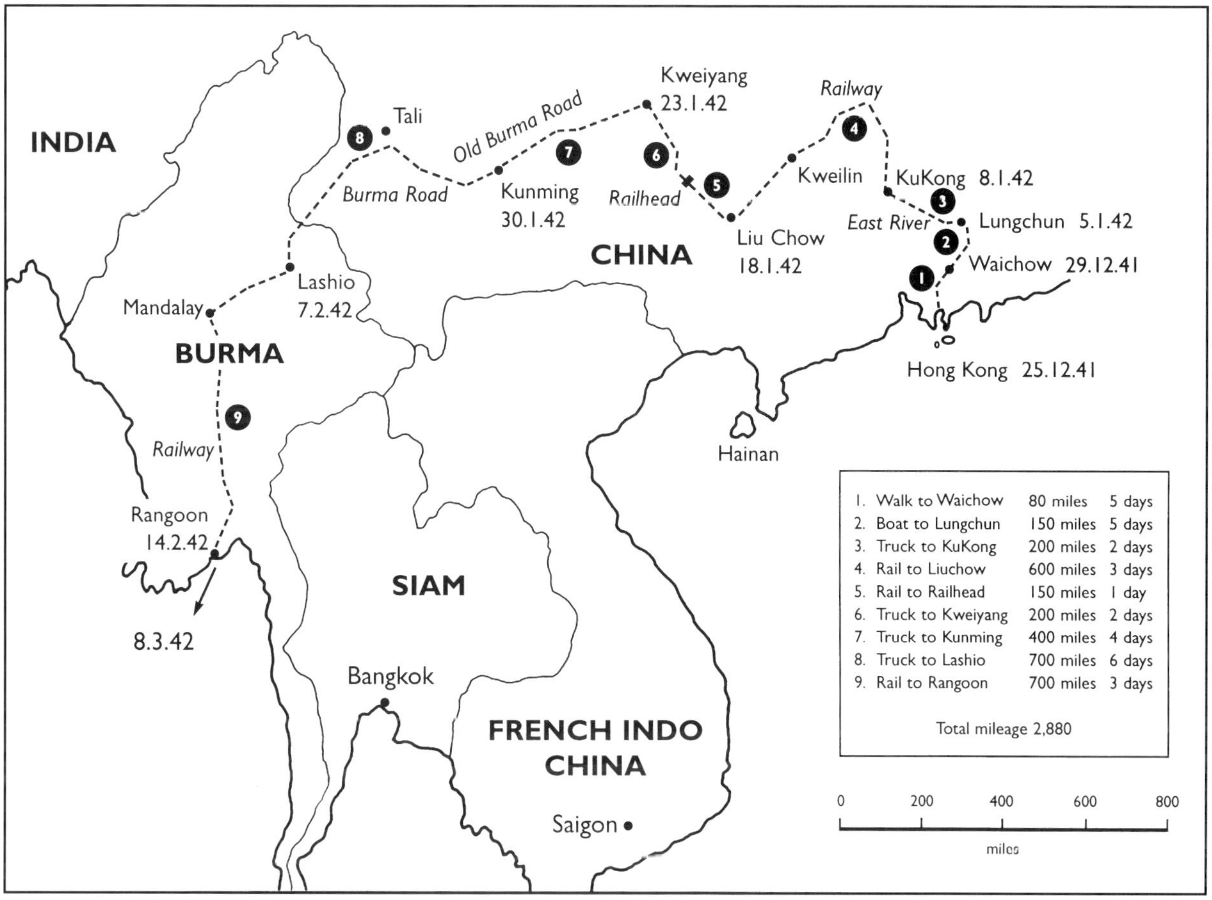

The 2nd MTB Flotilla's 'breakout from encirclement': Hong Kong to Rangoon, 25 December 1941 to 14 February 1942.

supplies—arms, ammunition, wireless sets and food. Then began the sad task of scuttling the five remaining boats of the flotilla. In deep water off the coast, holes were smashed in the bottom of each boat, the buoyant cushions slashed, and the sea-water intakes opened. There was no alternative—the boats did not have the range to reach any country as yet unoccupied by the Japanese, and they could not be allowed to fall into the enemy's hands.

When the men, sad faced and wretched, gathered on the shore, they found the party was now nearly seventy strong. It consisted of the Admiral and his staff of two, the three European guerrillas, eight officers and 36 men from the MTBs, and eighteen others—base staff, military staff and civilian officials. The Senior Naval Officer in Aberdeen, Commander Montague, with his staff, had been the last to escape in his tiny dockyard launch and had joined the group. By daybreak, a long straggling line of weary men was making its way inland from Namoa like packmules on a trail. By the time a halt was called near a tiny hamlet, many lessons had been learned. Packs were too heavy: unnecessary items had to be discarded. Everyone slept under trees after a welcome meal of steaming rice.

By mid-afternoon all were awake: it was a strange Boxing Day. The Hong Kong Volunteers—the experts—had been planning a route and preparing orders of advance. The first objective was Waichow, a town beyond the belt of Japanese occupied territory, some eighty miles away. First, two steep ridges had to be crossed—and fast progress had to be made to avoid interception by the enemy. Sleep by day and movement by night would prevent observation by aircraft. For the Admiral (to his disgust), a bamboo-pole sedan chair had been made to speed up progress, but almost all the party were totally untrained for this sort of operation and found it very hard going. Commander Montague, who was sixty years old, and others with wounds set an example of fortitude and determination which inspired the whole party.

The value of the presence of Admiral Chan Chak soon became apparent. It transpired that he was the President of the southern Kuomintang, the national party organisation in South China, and was a highly respected and a very popular figure in the area. This ensured that villagers along the way would produce green tea and rice to sustain the whole group.

Progress along very difficult paths, some no better than rocky water courses, was at first very slow, and a new hazard loomed ahead, a town well garrisoned by the Japanese. After fifteen hours and 31 miles the party was exhausted, but it was impossible to sleep due to intense cold. Next day Kendall, the European guerrilla who was guiding the party, pushed on again very fast for twelve miles, and then gave the welcome news that they had passed from occupied territory to an area under the influence of regular troops of Free China. They had been driven hard but expertly and had not seen a single Japanese.

On 29 December, with fourteen miles to go to Waichow, some bicycles were found for the older and less hardy, but the rest still walked. By 1600 all had reached the outskirts of Waichow and tea was provided before the party—escorted by a Chinese magistrate—attempted to march into the much-bombed city, with two nineteen-year-old MTB ratings carrying the White Ensign and the Chinese flag side by side. That evening there were comfortable beds and baths, and a banquet in true Chinese style—a huge contrast to the privations of the march. And in fact, the most physically gruelling part of the journey was over. Now staff work began to plan the succeeding stages of the very long way westward through China and Burma to the ultimate objective, the Naval base at Rangoon.

Crew of 09 at Waichow, 30 December 1941. Crew of 09 at Waichow, 30 December 1941. Left to right: [back row] Able Seaman Penny, Able Seaman Gurd, Telegraphist Hill, Able Seaman Hempenstall; [middle] Stoker Foster, Leading Seaman Schillemore (coxswain), Leading Stoker Priestly; [front] Sub-Lieutenant Brewer RHKNVR (First Lieutenant), Lieutenant Kennedy RNVR (Captain).

In this, Admiral Chan Chak was able to exert great influence and he was to accompany the party over the next two stages to KuKong. Until Waichow was reached, escape to rejoin British forces had been impossible to visualise, but now it became a reality. The people of Waichow were wonderfully hospitable, and before the party moved on, every member received gifts from children. They were not to know that only a month later, the town would be retaken by the Japanese.[5]

The next stage of the journey was up the East River for a hundred and fifty miles in two flat-bottomed motorboats towing two large sampans. It was not a straightforward passage: the engines of the boats, powered by ancient charcoal-gas systems, frequently broke down. Part of the reason for the breakdowns was the strain of towing the sampans, and it was no surprise when after one frustrating day the sampans were abandoned and everyone crowded into the motorboats. Safety levels were ignored, but progress improved.

Food was scarce and the ration was two bowls of soup per day. Again the Chinese in the villages demonstrated their hospitality: at the first real stop, the passengers poured ashore and were lavishly fed at no charge. They were met at their destination, Lung Chun, by the British Liaison Officer to the Chinese Army—an invaluable contact who was able to supply funds, and who took charge of details of the arrangements for the next stages. There was another civic reception with many speeches, and after a flowery welcome, Commander Montague, not to be outdone, ordered 'British will rise and bow three times to their Chinese allies!'

Then it was on to Stage 3—200 miles by truck to KuKong, the capital of the province since the Japanese occupation of Canton. As the road traversed a range of mountains with a highest pass of 5,000 feet, and the trucks were ancient and wildly driven, it was by no means a comfortable or trouble-free leg of the journey. Petrol was very scarce and negotiations for its purchase took hours. But the reception at KuKong was well up to standard: young girls pinned red favours on lapels proclaiming 'welcome to the glorious defenders of Hong Kong!' Embarrassed by this exuberance, the naval party did a token march for a few hundred yards before re-embarking and driving into the town. Banners welcoming Chan Chak and the party stretched across the streets.

Most of them were billeted aboard a large houseboat called the *Sea Palace*. It turned out later that they were temporary occupants of a Chinese 'flower-boat' or brothel.

They were presented to the Governor of the Province and to the Army Commander, General Yu Han Mow, and given first a banquet and, the next afternoon, a Grand Reception. The MTB men were keen to press on, and found a delay of another week very frustrating. The Admiral and his staff stayed at KuKong: the Admiral entered hospital to have the bullet lodged in his wrist removed, before taking up his next major appointment. Commander Montague and other staff officers flew to ChunKing, leaving the MTB men to go on to Rangoon.[6]

General Yu Han Mow with Admiral Chan Chak at KuKong.

Stage 4 was by train through the magnificent mountain country of the Canton-HanKow Railway. The map shows the tortuous nature of the line, northward and then south-westward to Luichow. There were frequent air raid warnings, but in three days the train covered 600 miles, a considerably better rate of progress than on most sections

Officers of the flotilla, with three daughters of Red Cross officials, at Kweiyang.

of the escape route. However, it took the train two more days to get out of the sidings before setting out for a railhead beyond which the line to Kweiyang was still being constructed. After that there was a further 200 mile section in four Chinese army trucks, two days of extreme discomfort and a great expenditure of nervous energy due to the techniques employed by the drivers.

This was a remote area of China, rarely visited by Westerners, and the countryside and people were very different in dress and customs, the roads primitive. One truck overturned when it skidded in the mud after continuous heavy rain. Five ratings were injured, but none seriously, and at least this led to a quick introduction at the hospital in Kweiyang to a uniformed Chinese officer wearing British medal ribbons from the 1914–1918 war. Dr Robert Lim spoke fluent English, was head of the Red Cross organisation in China, and had studied in Edinburgh and the United States before becoming a professor in Peking. He had married a Scotswoman, and had a 15-year-old daughter who acted as hostess to the British party during their two-day stay, which was memorable due to Dr Lim's kindness.

Kweiyang was at 4,000 feet altitude, and thereafter the route continued on the plateau. Gandy and the others had been moving for four weeks and were not even half way to Rangoon; the journey seemed interminable, but at least they were told that from this point, they were on a direct route towards Burma. The next objective, Kunming, was 400 miles away. When they reached this large and more prosperous town, they found a British Consul-General and evidence of contact with the British forces in Burma. Much of the news, however, was ominous, as the Japanese were themselves thrusting towards Rangoon from the north and it seemed that the men of the MTBs were engaged in another race against time in their bid for freedom. But as the road improved and higher speeds became possible, the 700 miles to Lashio were covered in just four days, despite delays at the Chinese/Burmese frontier.

Lashio was a railhead, and there the Naval party found signs of increasing pressure on the British in Burma. Timetables had been upset by the mass of people trying to get away from Rangoon, and the night train to the capital was several hours late in leaving. It was 14 February when they reached Rangoon, 51 days after they had left Hong Kong, and a journey of 2,880 miles was behind them. The first thing they heard was that Singapore had fallen. How long would it be before Rangoon fell too? And would they get out before it did? The evidence as they left the station was stark and disconcerting. The forecourt and the square were packed with Indians clamouring to leave. The city was clearly dying. There were none of the services that could have been expected in a major capital, and as a 'homecoming to freedom' the MTB men found it a terrible anti-climax.

For a brief period some of the officers and crew were allocated to launches and minesweepers of the Burma RNVR which were undermanned owning to desertions. Others helped to prepare for the evacuation of Rangoon, assisting in burning the files in the naval offices.

Lieutenant Commander Gandy and the members of the 2nd Flotilla who remained in Rangoon left for Calcutta aboard HMS *Jessen* on 8 March, and then sailed for Britain. Those at sea were collected at various ports on the Arakan coast, and most reached Calcutta. They took the train to Bombay and at last were bundled aboard the Cunard ship *Laconia* bound for home.

Further war service followed. Ron Ashby, (CO of MTB 07) who was awarded a DSC for his boat's attack on the Japanese landing craft on 19 December 1941, was briefly Senior Officer of a flotilla of 'D' Class Fairmile MTBs in the Mediterranean and went on to command the MLs in Burma. John Collingwood (MTB 11) also stayed in Coastal Forces, as Training Officer at Dover and later as SOO at HMS *Gregale* in Malta. Alexander Kennedy (MTB 09) spent two years as an instructor at HMS *St Christopher*, the Coastal forces training base at Fort William. In 1945 he had the remarkable experience of returning to Hong Kong soon after its recapture, when a Staff Officer aboard the aircraft carrier HMS *Pioneer*. He watched the arrival of Admiral Sir Bruce Fraser, Commander-in-Chief of the British Pacific Fleet, to receive the formal Japanese surrender at Government House.

Nothing certain is known of the fate of the ships' companies of MTBs 12 and 26, who were all listed as 'missing believed killed', nor of the officers and men of MTB 08, which was under repair in the dockyard at the time of the surrender and was destroyed. It is believed that the crew joined with the army in the final defence of the colony, and that many were killed.

Acknowledgements

The material upon which this article is based has two complementary sources. The first is the set of hand-written notes made by Lieutenant Commander G H Gandy RN during the attacks on Hong Kong and the journey through South China, accompanied by the reports he submitted on 8 March 1942 to C-in-C Far East on arrival in Rangoon. Copies of these were deposited at the Imperial War Museum by Lieutenant Commander Gandy's family.
The second is the privately published book *Hong Kong Full Circle 1939-1945* by Lieutenant Commander Alexander Kennedy VRD RNVR, the Commanding Officer of MTB 09, kindly made available to the author. It was written on his return to the UK at the end of the war in the Far East. A fuller account of the events described in this article will appear in the author's definitive history of the operations of MTBs in World War Two.

Notes

1. Adrian Rance, *Fast Boats and Flying Boats*, Ensign Publications, Southampton, 1989.
2. Lieutenant Commander Alexander Kennedy VRD RNVR (Retd), *Hong Kong Full Circle 1939–1945*. Privately published, 1969.
3. Lieutenant Commander G H Gandy RN, 'Report of Proceeding for the action on 19 December 1941 together with that of Lieutenant R R W Ashby RHNVR CO of MTB 07', written and submitted to C-in-C East Indies in March 1942 on reaching Rangoon.
4. Lieutenant Commander G H Gandy RN (Retd), Lieutenant A Kennedy RNVR and Lieutenant C J Collingwood RN, 'Reports of Proceedings for the later stages of the action on 19 December 1941', written and submitted as above.
5. Detail from (a) Lieutenant Commander G H Gandy, 'Reports of Proceedings from 8 December 1941 to 31 January', compiled from diary notes (held at Imperial War Museum) and written and submitted to C-in-C East Indies in March 1942 on reaching Rangoon; (b) Alexander Kennedy, op cit.
6. Little is known of Admiral Chan Chak's activities over the years 1942–1945, but when the Allies re-entered Hong Kong, it was learned that he had been appointed Mayor of Canton, the seat both of Government and Army Headquarters for the whole of southeast China.

The Imperial War Museum

The Imperial War Museum illustrates and records all aspects of the two world wars and other military operations involving Britain and the Commonwealth since 1914. The Museum, founded in 1917, was established by Act of Parliament in 1920 and has been in its present home (formerly the Bethlem Royal Hospital or Bedlam) since 1936. The Museum has three branches, HMS *Belfast*, Duxford and the Cabinet War Rooms. The Museum also occupies the former All Saints' Hospital, close to the Main Building, which houses a number of reference departments.

Research and Study Facilities

The Museum welcomes approaches from members of the public for research and study purposes. Its resources cover not only naval, military and air operations but also the social, political, economic and artistic aspects of conflict in the twentieth century.

Visitors intending to use the Museum's reference facilities should be aware that material of relevance to their fields of study may be found in more than one of the departments listed below. The leaflet, *Access to the Collections of the Imperial War Museum*, summarises holdings and facilities. More detailed information is available from individual departments.

Department of Art: twentieth century paintings, drawings and sculptures, posters, art medals and ephemera. The Department also holds the archive of correspondence with artists who were commissioned under the war artist schemes in the two world wars.

Department of Documents: primary source material, largely composed of British private papers and captured German records. It includes the papers of high-ranking officers such as Field Marshals Sir John French, Sir Henry Wilson and Viscount Montgomery of Alamein, manuscripts of the war poets and writers Isaac Rosenberg and Siegfried Sassoon and many personal diaries, letters and unpublished memoirs.

Department of Exhibits and Firearms: administers the Museum's collections of three-dimensional objects. Besides such larger exhibits as artillery, vehicles and small craft, most of which are displayed at Duxford near Cambridge, the holdings include uniforms, insignia, weapons, flags, communications equipment, models, medical equipment, cameras, toys, currency and ephemera.

Film and Video Archive: possibly the oldest in the world, with some 120 million feet of film, from the Boer War to Bosnia. Material by service cameramen, government-sponsored films, holdings from Allied and enemy sources, 'home movies' and television documentaries make a rich resource for history as captured by the 100-year-old medium of moving pictures.

Photograph Archive: a national archive of some five million photographs which includes the work of official military, professional and private photographers. Guides to various areas of the collection include a concise catalogue covering the First and Second World Wars. Lists of photographs on specific subjects are available and a catalogue of their titles can be sent on request.

Department of Printed Books: a national reference library comprising over 100,000 books as well as extensive collections of pamphlets, maps and technical drawings. In addition the Department holds important special collections, including those on women's activities during the First World War, aerial propaganda leaflets and ephemera such as song-sheets, stamps and theatre programmes.

Sound Archive: a national collection of over 26,000 hours of recorded material including retrospective interviews with service personnel and civilians and contemporary archive recordings such as speeches by well-known personalities, war reports and broadcasts, sound effects and war crimes trials; also radio programmes, lectures and poetry readings.

Opening hours

Reference Departments

Monday to Friday 10.00 am to 5.00 pm

At least 24 hours' notice should be given of an intended visit (for a visit to the Department of Art at least 48 hours' notice and for the Department of Film at least one week's notice is necessary).

Saturday 10.00 am to 5.00 pm

Departments of Documents and Printed Books only. A restricted service is offered on Saturday (except Bank Holiday weekends and the last two weekends of November). An appointment is essential since only pre-booked material can be made available and there is limired seating.

The Reference departments are closed on Public Holidays. The Departments of Documents and Printed Books are closed for the last two full weeks in November.

Imperial War Museum, Lambeth Road
London SE1 6HZ 0171-416 5000

Back numbers of the Imperial War Museum Review are available from:

Mail Order,
Imperial War Museum,
Duxford, Cambridge, CB2 4QR.

Payment must be made in sterling, either by international money order or a cheque drawn on a UK clearing bank. Access, Visa and Mastercard are also accepted. Telephone: 01223 835000 x245. Fax: 01223 837267. Details of trade information available on 0171-416 5396.

Review No 1 (published 1986)

Ronald Searle: war drawings 1939–45

A German cavalryman on the Eastern Front, 1915

The Kensingtons at Laventie: a twentieth century icon

Baltic Adventure: the exploits of CMB4, the coastal motorboat which torpedoed the Bolshevik cruiser *Oleg* in 1919

The provenance of a warship: the history of the design and building of HMS *Belfast*

'Geschäft Über Alles': notes on some medallions inspired by the sinking of the *Lusitania*

The illustrated First World War letters of the Reverend Canon Cyril Lomax

An introduction to the papers of Sir Henry Tizard

Spear against aeroplane: the making of Lutz Becker's film *Lion of Judah*

Tunisian Victory: a film too late?

'They are troops who fade, not flowers for poets' tearful fooling': Wilfred Owen and the nineteenth century romantic tradition

Revolutionary opposition to the Second World War

The Welsh Army Corps 1914–15: shortages of khaki and basic equipment promote a national uniform

The Steady Drummer (an essay on military history by Sir Brian Young)

Review No 2 (published 1987)

Photographers at Passchendaele

'It's not a bad life sometimes': Edward Ardizzone's drawings and paintings of the Second World War

'He acted what he sang': Gabriele D'Annunzio; poet, soldier and leader

British interception of German export newsreels, and the development of British combat filming, 1939–1942

Chinks in the armour: a study of seven propagandist themes as used on air-dropped leaflets

The Independent Labour Party contingent in the Spanish Civil War

'My Futile Mission': Captain Vernon Haggard and the Danube Flotilla, 1919

The Royal Navy and air power: the projected torpedo-bomber attack on the High Seas Fleet at Wilhelmshaven in 1918

Allied diplomacy and the Yugoslav question, 1943–1945

The Duxford Typhoon Wing 1941–1942

Ivor Gurney: 'Only the wanderer'

Four views of Normandy (a reflective piece by Sir Alan Harris)

Review No 3 (published 1988)

'A wonderful idea of the fighting': the question of fakes in *The Battle of the Somme*

The evacuation of Cape Helles, Gallipoli

Kamp Kufstein: a record of international refugee work in Austria during 1945

'*Vive La Nation*': French revolutionary themes in the posters and prints of the First World War

Night for day: the symbolic value of light in the painting of the Second World War

JW.53: convoy to Russia

'The Dead Man's Penny': a history of the Next of Kin memorial plaque

The Japanese Long Lance torpedo and its place in naval history

'*Swingmusik is verboten*': official policy towards popular music and 'dissident' youth in the Third Reich

'You smug-faced crowds': poetry on the Home Front in the First World War

'I know what it is to kill a pig; I won't kill a man': the Museum's oral history programme on conscientious objectors of the First World War

Change: some military consequences following the demise of our Indian Empire (by Colonel Brian Montgomery)

Review No 4 (published 1989)

Olive Edis: Imperial War Museum photographer in France and Belgium, March 1919

An introduction to the papers of Field Marshal Sir Henry Wilson

Images of war in Italy: the record made by the Army Film and Photographic Unit in Emilia Romagna, 1944–1945

An appreciation of the shelter photographs taken by Bill Brandt in November 1940

Moving images? The Parliamentary Recruiting Committee's poster campaign, 1914–1916

Des Illusions . . . Désillusions: an introduction to parties, personalities and posters in collaborationist France, 1940–1944

A gift for Christmas: the story of Princess Mary's Gift Fund, 1914

The German 'Biber' submarine

The trench raid at Chérisy, 15 September 1917

The loss of HMS *Hood*, 24 May 1941

The Ministry of Information and documentary film, 1939–1945

Review No 5 (published 1990)

Women in Munitions 1914–1918: the oral record

The Open Exhaust and some other trench journals of the First World War

The Liberation of Bergen–Belsen concentration camp in April 1945: the testimony of those involved

Henry Lamb and the First World War

'. . . And, if necessary, to carry it out': Operation 'Sealion' and the Black Book, fact and fiction

Small arms of Nationalist China 1937–1945

Film and reality: the *San Demetrio* episode

West Indians in Britain during the Second World War: a short history drawing on Colonial Office papers

The controversy over the use of dum dum bullets in the First World War

Review No 6 (published 1991)

Military mining on the Western Front

The writings of A B Austin, *Daily Herald* war correspondent

The First World War Women's Work Collection

The ethos of the British High Command, 1914–1918

Wyndham Lewis's war pictures

Bomber Command in the Battle of Britain

Christian iconography and First World War memorials

Americans in the Royal Flying Corps

Maurice Chevalier and charges of collaboration

Review No 7 (published 1992)

Army photographers in North-West Europe

Two Fusiliers: the First World War friendship of Robert Graves and Siegfried Sassoon

War propaganda and fascist myth: the poster collections of the Micheletti Foundation, Brescia

Early paintings of the Great War

'Keep smiling, keep those chins up and God Bless': filmed messages home from service personnel in the Far East during the Second World War

Post-war reconstruction as depicted in official British films of the Second World War

'Large Slow Targets': the Royal Navy's LST (2) Fleet in the Second World War

'The Number One Radio Personality of the War': Lord Haw Haw and his British audience during the Phoney War

The inevitable victory? El Alamein revisited

'The drama of the larder': Germany's food crisis 1914–1918

'The most lion-hearted man I ever met': Commander J W 'Tubby' Linton VC

Review No 8 (published 1993)

The end of the British Mandate in Palestine: reflections from the papers of John Watson, a member of the Forces Broadcasting Service

The British Pacific Fleet of 1944–45 and its newspaper, *Pacific Post*

'When d'you scarper? When d'you go into action? That's the nightmare!' The destruction of the South Nottinghamshire Hussars at Knightsbridge, 27 May – 6 June 1942

The war art of C R W Nevinson

The empty battlefield: the artist and landscape in the First World War

'Nobody's child': a brief history of the tactical use of Vickers machine-guns in the First World War

Too old or too bold? The removal of Sir Roger Keyes as Churchill's first Director of Combined Operations

Eton and the First World War

The German battlecruiser attack on the east coast ports, 16 December 1914

Review No 9 (published 1994)

George Rodger: gentleman, traveller and photographer

'A good bit of work': the Baltic diary of Commander Francis Goodhart DSO RN

The Whitehall Cenotaph: an accidental monument

Gassed and its detractors; interpreting Sargent's war painting

Unknown pioneer; Edward Foxen Cooper and the Imperial War Museum Film Archive, 1919–1934

Film as Allied assistance: Captain Bromhead's mission to Russia, 1916–1917

'A bit of campaign oratory': Wendell Willkie's visit to Britain, January 1941, and the fight for Lend–Lease

Somme footnote; the Battle of the Ancre and the struggle for Frankfort Trench, November 1916

Review No 10 (published 1995)

Working class women's service newspapers and the First World War

The myths of Langemarck

Becker's monsters: German hybrid artillery and Operation 'Goodwood'

'When all is said and done, we are here solely for their benefit . . .': the British Naval Mission in North Russia, 1941–1945

The Caquot balloon

Tales from 'the bushy-topped tree': a brief survey of military sketching

Operation 'Union': British families in Germany, 1946

The Great Landing: Haig's plan to invade Belgium from the sea in 1917

General Harper and the failure of 51st (Highland) Division at Cambrai, 20 November 1917

Some near misses in the Second World War (The Birley Memorial Lecture 1994)